THE ILLUSTRATED

LARK RISE TO CANDLEFORD

FLORA THOMPSON

Flora Thompson's trilogy *Lark Rise to Candleford* is one of the best-loved of all books about the English countryside. It was published forty years ago, and the past it describes is now a century away. Yet it remains perhaps the most vivid, detailed and immediate portrait of country life ever written.

Flora Thompson herself was a cottage child, born in 1877 and brought up in poverty in the tiny Oxfordshire hamlet of Juniper. (Juniper is renamed Lark Rise in the book, and Flora calls herself Laura.) From the age of five to when she left school at twelve, she and her brothers and sisters walked each day the three miles to Cottisford (Fordlow), where her teacher Miss Holmes used to say, 'Oh, Laura! What a dunce you are!' But Miss Holmes was wrong, for Flora possessed the literary gifts, the eye and memory for everyday detail and the intimacies of experience, which would one day combine to produce this gentle masterpiece.

In the 1880s the countryside was on the brink of unalterable change, and the march of progress would soon wipe away the unique idiosyncrasies of a centuries-old way of life. But Flora Thompson was born in time to capture it before it vanished for ever, with her unforgettable gallery of characters – Old Sally, Miss Lane the postmistress, Sir Timothy, Miss Macey and the rest – and her unsentimental but deeply affectionate account of the humble details of the life she knew.

THE ILLUSTRATED
LARK RISE TO CANDLEFORD

A TRILOGY BY FLORA THOMPSON

ABRIDGED BY JULIAN SHUCKBURGH

BOOK CLUB ASSOCIATES · LONDON

First published in this edition 1983 by
Book Club Associates
by arrangement with
Century Publishing Co Ltd

Lark Rise was first published by
Oxford University Press in 1939; *Over to
Candleford* in 1941; and *Candleford Green*
in 1943. Issued together under the title
Lark Rise to Candleford in 1945

This edition designed and produced by
Shuckburgh Reynolds Limited
8 Northumberland Place, London W2 5BS

Designed by Nicholas Thirkell
Assistant designers:
Bob Rowinski and Paul Fielding
Picture research by Jenny de Gex

Typeset in 13 point Ehrhardt by
SX Composing Limited, Rayleigh, Essex

Printed and bound in the Netherlands by
Drukkerij de Lange/van Leer bv, Deventer

CN 5206

CONTENTS

LARK RISE

OVER TO CANDLEFORD

CANDLEFORD GREEN

LARK RISE

——— I ———

A HAMLET CHILDHOOD

THE hamlet stood on a gentle rise in the flat, wheat-growing north-east corner of Oxfordshire. We will call it Lark Rise because of the great number of skylarks which made the surrounding fields their springboard and nested on the bare earth between the rows of green corn.

All around, from every quarter, the stiff, clayey soil of the arable fields crept up; bare, brown and windswept for eight months out of the twelve. Spring brought a flush of green wheat and there were violets under the hedges and pussy-willows out beside the brook at the bottom of the 'Hundred Acres'; but only for a few weeks in later summer had the landscape real beauty. Then the ripened cornfields rippled up to the doorsteps of the cottages and the hamlet became an island in a sea of dark gold.

To a child it seemed that it must always have been so; but the ploughing and sowing and reaping were recent innovations. Old men could remember when the Rise, covered with juniper bushes, stood in the midst of a furzy heath – common land, which had come under the plough after the passing of the Enclosure Acts. Some of the ancients still occupied cottages on land which had been ceded to their fathers as 'squatters' rights', and probably all the small plots upon which the houses stood had originally been so ceded. In the eighteen-eighties the hamlet consisted of about thirty cottages and an inn, not built in rows, but dotted down anywhere within a more or less circular group. A deeply rutted cart track surrounded the whole, and separate houses or groups of houses were connected by a network of pathways. Going from one part of the hamlet to another was called 'going round the Rise', and the plural of 'house' was not 'houses', but 'housen'. The only shop was a small general one kept in the back kitchen of the inn. The church and school were in the mother village, a mile and a half away.

A road flattened the circle at one point. It had been cut when the heath was enclosed, for convenience in fieldwork and to connect the main Oxford road with the mother village and a series of other villages beyond. From the hamlet it led on the one hand to church and school, and on the other to the main road, or the turnpike, as it was still called, and so to the market town where the Saturday shopping was done. It brought little traffic past the hamlet. An occasional farm wagon, piled with sacks or square-cut bundles of hay; a farmer on horseback or in his gig; the baker's little old white-tiled van; a string of blanketed hunters with grooms, exercising in the early morning; and a carriage with gentry out paying calls in the afternoon were about the sum of it. No motors, no buses, and only one of the old penny-farthing high bicycles at rare intervals. People still rushed to their cottage doors to see one of the latter come past.

A few of the houses had thatched roofs, whitewashed outer walls and diamond-paned windows, but the majority were just stone or brick boxes with blue-slated roofs. The older houses were relics of pre-enclosure days and were still occupied by descendants of the original squatters, themselves at that time elderly people. One old couple owned a donkey and cart, which they used to carry their vegetables, eggs, and honey to the market town and sometimes hired out at sixpence a day to their neighbours. One house was occupied by a retired farm bailiff, who was reported to have 'well feathered his own nest' during his years of stewardship. Another aged man owned and worked upon about an acre of land. These, the innkeeper, and one other man, a stonemason who walked the three miles to and from his work in the town every day, were the only ones not employed as agricultural labourers.

Some of the cottages had two bedrooms, others only one, in which case it had to be divided by a screen or curtain to accommodate parents and children. Often the big boys of a family slept downstairs, or were put out to sleep in the second bedroom of an elderly couple whose own children were out in the world. Except at holiday times, there were no big girls to provide for, as they were all out in service. Still, it was often a tight fit, for children swarmed, eight, ten, or even more in some families, and although they were seldom all at home together, the eldest often being married before the youngest was born, beds and shakedowns were often so closely packed that the inmates had to climb over one bed to get into another. . . .

In nearly all the cottages there was but one room downstairs, and many of these were poor and bare, with only a table and a few chairs and stools for furniture and a superannuated potato-sack thrown down by way of hearthrug. Other rooms were bright and cosy, with dressers of crockery, cushioned

9

chairs, pictures on the walls and brightly coloured hand-made rag rugs on the floor. In these there would be pots of geraniums, fuchsias, and old-fashioned sweet-smelling musk on the windowsills. In the older cottages there were grandfathers' clocks, gate-legged tables, and rows of pewter, relics of a time when life was easier for country folk.

The interiors varied, according to the number of mouths to be fed and the thrift and skill of the housewife, or the lack of those qualities; but the income in all was precisely the same, for ten shillings a week was the standard wage of the farm labourer at that time in that district.

Looking at the hamlet from a distance, one house would have been seen, a little apart, and turning its back on its neighbours, as though about to run away into the fields. It was a small grey stone cottage with a thatched roof, a green-painted door and

a plum tree trained up the wall to the eaves. This was called the 'end house' and was the home of the stonemason and his family. At the beginning of the decade there were two children: Laura, aged three, and Edmund, a year and a half younger. In some respects these children, while small, were more fortunate than their neighbours. Their father earned a little more money than the labourers. Their mother had been a children's nurse and they were well looked after. They were taught good manners and taken for walks, milk was bought for them, and they were bathed regularly on Saturday nights and, after 'Gentle Jesus' was said, were tucked up in bed with a peppermint or clove ball to suck. They had tidier clothes, too, for their mother had taste and skill with her needle and better-off relations sent them parcels of outgrown clothes. The other children used to tease the little girl about the lace on her drawers and led her such a life that she once took them off and hid them in a haystack. . . .

The first charge on the labourers' ten shillings was house rent. Most of the cottages belonged to small tradesmen in the market town and the weekly rents ranged from one shilling to half a crown. Some labourers in other villages worked on farms or estates where they had their cottages rent free; but the hamlet people did not envy them, for 'Stands to reason,' they said, 'they've allus got to do just what they be told, or out they goes, neck and crop, bag and baggage.' A shilling, or even two shillings a week, they felt, was not too much to pay for the freedom to live and vote as they liked and to go to church or chapel or neither as they preferred.

Every house had a good vegetable garden and there were allotments for all; but only three of the thirty cottages had their own water supply. The less fortunate tenants obtained their water from a well on a vacant plot on the outskirts of the hamlet, from which the cottage had disappeared. There was no public well or pump. They just had to get their water where and how they could; the landlords did not undertake to supply water.

Against the wall of every well-kept cottage stood a tarred or green-painted water butt to catch and store the rain-water from the roof. This saved many journeys to the well with buckets, as it could be used for cleaning and washing clothes and for watering small, precious things in the garden. It was also valued for toilet purposes and women would hoard the last drops for themselves and their children to wash in. Rain-water was supposed to be good for the complexion, and, though they had no money to spend upon beautifying themselves, they were not too far gone in poverty to neglect such means as they had to that end.

For drinking water, and for cleaning water, too, when the water butts failed, the women went to the well in all weathers, drawing up the buckets with a windlass and carting them home suspended from their shoulders by a yoke. Those were weary

journeys 'round the Rise' for water, and many were the rests and endless was the gossip, as they stood at corners in their big white aprons and crossover shawls. . . .

In dry summers, when the hamlet wells failed, water had to be fetched from a pump at some farm buildings half a mile distant. Those who had wells in their gardens would not give away a spot, as they feared if they did theirs, too, would run dry, so they fastened down the lids with padlocks and disregarded all hints.

The only sanitary arrangement known in the hamlet was housed either in a little beehive-shaped building at the bottom of the garden or in a corner of the wood and toolshed known as 'the hovel'. It was not even an earth closet; but merely a deep pit with a seat set over it, the half-yearly emptying of which caused every door and window in the vicinity to be sealed. Unfortunately, there was no means of sealing the chimneys!

The 'privies' were as good an index as any to the characters of their owners. Some

were horrible holes; others were fairly decent, while some, and these not a few, were kept well cleared, with the seat scrubbed to snow-whiteness and the brick floor raddled. One old woman even went so far as to nail up a text as a finishing touch, 'Thou God seest me' – most embarrassing to a Victorian child who had been taught that no one must even see her approach the door.

In other such places health and sanitary maxims were scrawled with lead pencil or yellow chalk on the whitewashed walls. Most of them embodied sound sense and some were expressed in sound verse, but few were so worded as to be printable. One short and pithy maxim may pass: 'Eat well, work well, sleep well, and – well once a day.' . . .

At the back or side of each cottage was a lean-to pigsty and the house refuse was thrown on a nearby pile called 'the muck'll'. This was so situated that the oozings from the sty could drain into it; the manure was also thrown there when the sty was cleared, and the whole formed a nasty, smelly eyesore to have within a few feet of the windows.

'The wind's in the so-and-so,' some woman indoors would say, 'I can smell th' muck'll,' and she would often be reminded of the saying, 'Pigs for health', or told that the smell was a healthy one.

It was in a sense a healthy smell for them; for a good pig fattening in the sty promised a good winter. During its lifetime the pig was an important member of the family, and its health and condition were regularly reported in letters to children away from home, together with news of their brothers and sisters. Men callers on Sunday afternoons came, not to see the family, but the pig, and would lounge with its owner against the pigsty door for an hour, scratching piggy's back and praising his points or turning up their own noses in criticism.

Ten to fifteen shillings was the price paid for a pigling when weaned, and they all delighted in getting a bargain. Some men swore by the 'dilling', as the smallest of a litter was called, saying it was little and good, and would soon catch up; others preferred to give a few shillings more for a larger young pig.

The family pig was everybody's pride and everybody's business. Mother spent hours boiling up the 'little taturs' to mash and mix with the pot-liquor, in which food had been cooked, to feed to the pig for its evening meal and help out the expensive barley meal. The children, on their way home from school, would fill their arms with sow thistle, dandelion, and choice long grass, or roam along the hedgerows on wet evenings collecting snails in a pail for the pig's supper. These piggy crunched up with great relish. 'Feyther', over and above farming out the sty, bedding down, doctoring, and so on, would even go without his nightly half-pint when, towards the end, the barley-meal mounted until 'it fair frightened anybody'.

Sometimes, when the weekly income would not run to a sufficient quantity of fattening food, an arrangement would be made with the baker or miller that he should give credit now, and when the pig was killed receive a portion of the meat in payment. More often than not one-half the pig-meat would be mortgaged in this way, and it was no uncommon thing to hear a woman say, 'Us be going to kill half a pig, please God, come Friday,' leaving the uninitiated to conclude that the other half would still run about in the sty.

Some of the families killed two separate half pigs a year; others one, or even two, whole ones, and the meat provided them with bacon for the winter or longer. Fresh meat was a luxury only seen in a few of the cottages on Sunday, when sixpennyworth of pieces would be bought to make a meat pudding. If a small joint came their way as a Saturday night bargain, those without oven grates would roast it by suspending it on a string before the fire, with one of the children in attendance as turnspit. Or a 'pot-roast' would be made by placing the meat with a little lard or other fat in an iron saucepan and keeping it well shaken over the fire. But, after all, as they said, there was nothing to beat a 'toad'. For this the meat was enclosed whole in a suet crust and well boiled, a method which preserved all the delicious juices of the meat and provided a good pudding into the bargain. When some superior person tried to give them a hint, the women used to say, 'you tell us how to get the victuals; we can cook it all right when we've got it'; and they could.

When the pig was fattened – and the fatter the better – the date of execution had to be decided upon. It had to take place some time during the first two quarters of the moon; for, if the pig was killed when the moon was waning the bacon would shrink in cooking, and they wanted it to 'plimp up'. The next thing was to engage the travelling pork butcher, or pig-sticker, and, as he was a thatcher by day, he always had to kill after dark, the scene being lighted with lanterns and the fire of burning straw which at a later stage of the proceedings was to singe the bristles off the victim.

The killing was a noisy, bloody business, in the course of which the animal was hoisted to a rough bench that it might bleed thoroughly and so preserve the quality of the meat. The job was often bungled, the pig sometimes getting away and having to be chased; but country people of that day had little sympathy for the sufferings of animals, and men, women, and children would gather round to see the sight.

After the carcass had been singed, the pig-sticker would pull off the detachable, gristly, outer coverings of the toes, known locally as 'the shoes', and fling them among the children, who scrambled for, then sucked and gnawed them, straight from the filth of the sty and blackened by fire as they were.

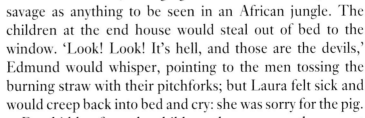

The whole scene, with its mud and blood, flaring lights and dark shadows, was as savage as anything to be seen in an African jungle. The children at the end house would steal out of bed to the window. 'Look! Look! It's hell, and those are the devils,' Edmund would whisper, pointing to the men tossing the burning straw with their pitchforks; but Laura felt sick and would creep back into bed and cry: she was sorry for the pig.

But, hidden from the children, there was another aspect of the pig-killing. Months of hard work and self-denial were

15

brought on that night to a successful conclusion. It was a time to rejoice, and rejoice they did, with beer flowing freely and the first delicious dish of pig's fry sizzling in the frying-pan.

The next day, when the carcass had been cut up, joints of pork were distributed to those neighbours who had sent similar ones at their own pig-killing. Small plates of fry and other oddments were sent to others as a pure compliment, and no one who happened to be ill or down on his luck at these occasions was ever forgotten.

Then the housewife 'got down to it', as she said. Hams and sides of bacon were salted, to be taken out of the brine later and hung on the wall near the fireplace to dry. Lard was dried out, hog's puddings were made, and the chitterlings were cleaned and turned three days in succession under running water, according to ancient ritual. It was a busy time, but a happy one, with the larder full and something over to give away, and all the pride and importance of owning such riches.

On the following Sunday came the official 'pig feast', when fathers and mothers, sisters and brothers, married children and grandchildren who lived within walking distance arrived to dinner.

If the house had no oven, permission was obtained from an old couple in one of the thatched cottages to heat up the big bread-baking oven in their wash-house. This was like a large cupboard with an iron door, lined with brick and going far back into the wall. Faggots of wood were lighted inside and the door was closed upon them until the oven was well heated. Then the ashes were swept out and baking tins with joints of pork, potatoes, batter puddings, pork pies, and sometimes a cake or two, were popped inside and left to bake without further attention.

Meanwhile, at home, three or four different kinds of vegetables would be cooked, and always a meat pudding, made in a basin. No feast and few Sunday dinners were considered complete without that item, which was eaten alone, without vegetables, when a joint was to follow. On ordinary days the pudding would be a roly-poly containing fruit, currants, or jam; but it still appeared as a first course, the idea being that it took the edge off the appetite. At the pig feast there would be no sweet pudding, for that could be had any day, and who wanted sweet things when there was plenty of meat to be had!

But this glorious plenty only came once or at most twice a year, and there were all the other days to provide for. How was it done on ten shillings a week? Well, for one thing, food was much cheaper than it is today. Then, in addition to the bacon, all vegetables, including potatoes, were home-grown and grown in abundance. The men took great pride in their gardens and allotments and there was always competition amongst them as to who should have the earliest and choicest of each kind. Fat green peas, broad beans as big as a halfpenny, cauliflowers a child could make an armchair of, runner beans and cabbage and kale, all in their seasons went into the pot with the roly-poly and slip of bacon.

Then they ate plenty of green food, all home-grown and freshly pulled; lettuce and radishes and young onions with pearly heads and leaves like fine grass. A few slices of bread and home-made lard, flavoured with rosemary, and plenty of green food 'went down good' as they used to say.

Bread had to be bought, and that was a heavy item, with so many growing children to be fed; but flour for the daily pudding and an occasional plain cake could be laid in for the winter without any cash outlay. After the harvest had been carried from the fields, the women and children swarmed over the stubble picking up the ears of wheat the horse-rake had missed. Gleaning, or 'leazing', as it was called locally.

Up and down and over and over the stubble they hurried, backs bent, eyes on the ground, one hand outstretched to pick up the ears, the other resting on the small of the back with the 'handful'. When this had been completed, it was bound round with a wisp of straw and erected with others in a double rank, like the harvesters erected their sheaves in shocks, beside the leazer's water-can and dinner-basket. It was hard work, from as soon as possible after daybreak until nightfall, with only two short breaks for refreshment; but the single ears mounted, and a woman with four or five strong, well-disciplined children would carry a good load home on the head every night. And they enjoyed doing it, for it was pleasant in the fields under the pale blue August sky, with the clover springing green in the stubble and the hedges bright with hips and haws and feathery with traveller's joy. When the rest-hour came, the children would wander off down the hedgerows gathering crab-apples or sloes, or searching for mushrooms, while the mothers reclined and suckled their babes and drank their cold tea and gossiped or dozed until it was time to be at it again.

At the end of the fortnight or three weeks that the leazing lasted, the corn would be thrashed out at home and sent to the miller, who paid himself for grinding by taking toll of the flour. Great was the excitement in a good year when the flour came home – one bushel, two bushels, or even more in large, industrious families. The mealy-white sack with its contents was often kept for a time on show on a chair in the living-room and it was a common thing for a passer-by to be invited to 'step inside an' see our little bit o' leazings'. They liked to have the product of their labour before their own eyes and to let others admire it, just as the artist likes to show his picture and the composer to hear his opus played. 'Them's better'n any o' yer oil-paintin's,' a man would say, pointing to the flitches on his wall, and the women felt the same about the leazings.

Here, then, were the three chief ingredients of the one hot meal a day, bacon from the flitch, vegetables from the garden, and flour for the roly-poly. This meal, called 'tea', was taken in the evening, when the men were home from the fields and the children from school, for neither could get home at midday.

About four o'clock, smoke would go up from the chimneys, as the fire was made up and the big iron boiler, or the three-legged pot, was slung on the hook of the chimney-chain. Everything was cooked in the one utensil; the square of bacon, amounting to little more than a taste each; cabbage, or other green vegetables in one net, potatoes in another, and the roly-poly swathed in a cloth. It sounds a haphazard

method in these days of gas and electric cookers; but it answered its purpose, for, by carefully timing the putting in of each item and keeping the simmering of the pot well regulated, each item was kept intact and an appetising meal was produced. The water in which the food had been cooked, the potato parings, and other vegetable trimmings were the pig's share.

When the men came home from work they would find the table spread with a clean whitey-brown cloth, upon which would be knives and two-pronged steel forks with buckhorn handles. The vegetables would then be turned out into big round yellow crockery dishes and the bacon cut into dice, with much the largest cube upon Feyther's plate, and the whole family would sit down to the chief meal of the day. True, it was seldom that all could find places at the central table; but some of the smaller children could sit upon stools with the seat of a chair for a table, or on the doorstep with their plates on their laps.

Good manners prevailed. The children were given their share of the food, there was no picking and choosing, and they were expected to eat it in silence. 'Please' and 'Thank you' were permitted, but nothing more. Father and Mother might talk if they wanted to; but usually they were content to concentrate upon their enjoyment of the meal. Father might shovel green peas into his mouth with his knife, Mother might drink her tea from her saucer, and some of the children might lick their plates when the food was devoured; but who could eat peas with a two-pronged fork, or wait for tea to cool after the heat and flurry of cooking, and licking the plates passed as a graceful compliment to Mother's good dinner. 'Thank God for my good dinner. Thank Father and Mother. Amen' was the grace used in one family, and it certainly had the merit of giving credit where credit was due.

For other meals they depended largely on bread and butter, or, more often, bread

and lard, eaten with any relish that happened to be at hand. Fresh butter was too costly for general use, but a pound was sometimes purchased in the summer, when it cost tenpence. Margarine, then called 'butterine', was already on the market, but was little used there, as most people preferred lard, especially when it was their own home-made lard flavoured with rosemary leaves. In summer there was always plenty of green food from the garden and home-made jam as long as it lasted, and sometimes an egg or two, where fowls were kept, or when eggs were plentiful and sold at twenty a shilling.

When bread and lard appeared alone, the men would spread mustard on their slices and the children would be given a scraping of black treacle or a sprinkling of brown sugar. Some children, who preferred it, would have 'sop' – bread steeped in boiling water, then strained and sugar added.

Milk was a rare luxury, as it had to be fetched a mile and a half from the farmhouse. The cost was not great: a penny a jug or can, irrespective of size. It was, of course, skimmed milk, but hand-skimmed, not separated, and so still had some small propor-tion of cream left. A few families fetched it daily; but many did not bother about it. The women said they preferred their tea neat, and it did not seem to occur to them that the children needed milk. Many of them never tasted it from the time they were weaned until they went out in the world. Yet they were stout-limbed and rosy-cheeked and full of life and mischief.

'Poverty's no disgrace, but 'tis a great inconvenience' was a common saying among the Lark Rise people; but that put the case too mildly, for their poverty was no less than a hampering drag upon them. Everybody had enough to eat and a shelter which, though it fell far short of modern requirements, satisfied them. Coal at a shilling a hundredweight and a pint of paraffin for lighting *had* to be squeezed out of the weekly wage; but for boots, clothes, illness, holidays, amusements, and household renewals there was no provision whatever. How did they manage?

Boots were often bought with the extra money the men earned in the harvest field. When that was paid, those lucky families which were not in arrears with their rent would have a new pair all round, from the father's hobnailed dreadnoughts to little pink kid slippers for the baby. Then some careful housewives paid a few pence every week into the boot club run by a shopkeeper in the market town. This helped; but it was not sufficient, and how to get a pair of new boots for 'our young Ern or Alf' was a problem which kept many a mother awake at night.

Girls needed boots, too, and good, stout, nailed ones for those rough and muddy roads; but they were not particular, any boots would do. At a confirmation class which Laura attended, the clergyman's daughter, after weeks of careful preparation, asked her catechumens: 'Now, are you sure you are all of you thoroughly prepared for tomorrow. Is there anything you would like to ask me?'

'Yes, miss,' piped up a voice in a corner, 'me mother says have you got a pair of your old boots you could give me, for I haven't got any fit to go in.'

Alice got her boots on that occasion; but there was not a confirmation every day. Still, boots were obtained somehow; nobody went barefoot, even though some of the toes might sometimes stick out beyond the toe of the boot.

To obtain clothes was an even more difficult matter. Mothers of families sometimes said in despair that they supposed they would have to black their own backsides and go naked. They never quite came to that; but it was difficult to keep decently covered, and that was a pity because they did dearly love what they called 'anything a bit dressy'. This taste was not encouraged by the garments made by the girls in school from material given by the Rectory people – roomy chemises and wide-legged drawers made of unbleached calico, beautifully sewn, but without an inch of trimming; harsh, but strong flannel petticoats and worsted stockings that would almost stand up with no legs in them – although these were

gratefully received and had their merits, for they wore for years and the calico improved with washing.

For outer garments they had to depend upon daughters, sisters, and aunts away in service, who all sent parcels, not only of their own clothes, but also of those they could beg from their mistresses. These were worn and altered and dyed and turned and ultimately patched and darned as long as the threads hung together.

But, in spite of their poverty and the worry and anxiety attending it, they were not unhappy, and, though poor, there was nothing sordid about their lives. 'The nearer the bone the sweeter the meat', they used to say, and they were getting very near the bone from which their country ancestors had fed. Their children and children's children would have to depend wholly upon whatever was carved for them from the communal joint, and for their pleasure upon the mass enjoyments of a new era. But for that generation there was still a small picking left to supplement the weekly wage. They had their home-cured bacon, their 'bit o' leazings', their small wheat or barley patch on the allotment; their knowledge of herbs for their homely simples, and the wild fruits and berries of the countryside for jam, jellies, and wine, and round about them as part of their lives were the last relics of country customs and the last echoes of country songs, ballads, and game rhymes. This last picking, though meagre, was sweet.

Oxford was only nineteen miles distant. The children at the end house knew that, for, while they were small, they were often taken by their mother for a walk along the turnpike and would never pass the milestone until the inscription had been read to them: OXFORD XIX MILES.

They often wondered what Oxford was like and asked questions about it. One answer was that it was 'a gert big town' where a man might earn as much as five and twenty shillings a week; but as he would have to pay 'pretty near' half of it in house rent and have nowhere to keep a pig or to grow many vegetables, he'd be a fool to go there.

One girl who had actually been there on a visit said you could buy a long stick of pink-and-white rock for a penny and that one of her aunt's young gentlemen lodgers had given her a whole shilling for cleaning his shoes. Their mother said it was called a city because a bishop lived there, and that a big fair was held there once a year, and that was all she seemed to know about it. They did not ask their father, although he had lived there as a child, when his parents had kept an hotel in the city (his relations spoke of it as an hotel, but his wife once called it a pot-house, so probably it was an ordinary public-house). They already had to be careful not to ask their father too many questions, and when their mother said, 'Your father's cross again', they found it was better not to talk at all.

So, for some time, Oxford remained to them a dim blur of bishops (they had seen a picture of one with big white sleeves, sitting in a high-backed chair) and swings and shows and coconut shies (for they knew what a fair was like) and little girls sucking pink-and-white rock and polishing shoes. To imagine a place without pigsties and vegetable gardens was more difficult. With no bacon or cabbage, what could people have to eat?

But the Oxford road with the milestone they had known as long as they could remember. Round the Rise and up the narrow hamlet road they would go until they came to the turning, their mother pushing the baby carriage ('pram' was a word of the future) with Edmund strapped in the high, slippery seat, or, later, little May, who was born when Edmund was five, and Laura holding on at the side or darting hither and thither to pick flowers. . . .

The white tails of rabbits bobbed in and out of the hedgerows; stoats crossed the road in front of the children's feet – swift, silent, stealthy creatures which made them shudder; there were squirrels in the oak-trees, and once they even saw a fox curled up asleep in the ditch beneath thick overhanging ivy. Bands of little blue butterflies flitted here and there or poised themselves with quivering wings on the long grass bents; bees hummed in the white clover blooms, and over all a deep silence brooded. It seemed as though the road had been made ages before, then forgotten.

The children were allowed to run freely on the grass verges, as wide as a small meadow in places. 'Keep to the grinsard,' their mother would call. 'Don't go on the road. Keep to the grinsard!' and it was many years before Laura realized that that name for the grass verges, in general use there, was a worn survival of the old English 'greensward'.

It was no hardship for her to be obliged to keep to the greensward, for flowers strange to the hamlet soil flourished there, eyebright and harebell, sunset-coloured patches of lady's-glove, and succory with vivid blue flowers and stems like black wire. . . .

It was while they were still small they were walking there one day with a visiting aunt; Edmund and Laura, both in clean, white, starched clothes, holding on to a hand on either side. The children were a little shy, for they did not remember seeing this aunt before. She was married to a master builder in Yorkshire and only visited her brother and his family at long intervals. But they liked her, although Laura had already sensed that their mother did not. Jane was too dressy and 'set up' for her taste, she said. That morning, her luggage being still at the railway station, she was wearing the clothes she had travelled in, a long, pleated dove-coloured gown with an apron arrangement drawn round and up and puffed over a bustle at the back, and, on her head, a tiny toque made entirely of purple velvet pansies.

25

Swish, swish, swish, went her long skirt over the grass verges; but every time they crossed the road she would relinquish Laura's hand to gather it up from the dust, thus revealing to the child's delighted gaze a frilly purple petticoat. When she was grown up she would have a frock and petticoat just like those, she decided.

But Edmund was not interested in clothes. Being a polite little boy, he was trying to make conversation. He had already shown his aunt the spot where they had found the dead hedgehog and the bush where the thrush had built last spring and told her the distant rumble they heard was a train going over the viaduct, when they came to the milestone.

'Aunt Jenny,' he said, 'what's Oxford like?'

'Well, it's all old buildings, churches and colleges where rich people's sons go to school when they're grown up.'

'What do they learn there?' demanded Laura.

'Oh, Latin and Greek and suchlike, I suppose.'

'Do they all go there?' asked Edmund seriously.

'Well, no. Some go to Cambridge; there are colleges there as well. Some go to one and some to the other,' said the aunt with a smile that meant 'Whatever will these children want to know next?'

Four-year-old Edmund pondered a few moments, then said, 'Which college shall I go to when I am grown up, Oxford or Cambridge?' and his expression of innocent good faith checked his aunt's inclination to laugh.

'There won't be any college for you, my poor little man,' she explained. 'You'll have to go to work as soon as you leave school; but if I could have *my* way, you should go to the very best college in Oxford,' and, for the rest of the walk she entertained them with stories of her mother's family, the Wallingtons.

She said one of her uncles had written a book and she thought Edmund might turn out to be clever, like him. But when they told their mother what she had said she tossed her head and said she had never heard about any book, and what if he had, wasting his time. It was not as if he was like Shakespeare or Miss Braddon or anybody like that. And she hoped Edmund would not turn out to be clever. Brains were no good to a working man; they only made him discontented and saucy and lose his jobs. She'd seen it happen again and again.

Yet she had brains of her own and her education had been above the average in her station in life. She had been born and brought up in a cottage standing in the churchyard of a neighbouring village, 'just like the little girl in *We are Seven*', she used to tell her own children. At the time when she was a small girl in the churchyard cottage the incumbent of the parish had been an old man and with him had lived his still more aged sister. This lady, whose name was Miss Lowe, had become very fond of the pretty, fair-haired little girl at the churchyard cottage and had had her at the Rectory

every day out of school hours. Little Emma had a sweet voice and she was supposed to go there for singing lessons; but she had learned other things, too, including old-world manners and to write a beautiful antique hand with delicate, open-looped pointed letters and long 's's', such as her instructress and other young ladies had been taught in the last quarter of the eighteenth century.

Miss Lowe was then nearly eighty, and had long been dead when Laura, at two and a half years old, had been taken by her mother to see the by then very aged Rector. The visit was one of her earliest memories, which survived as an indistinct impression of twilight in a room with dark green walls and the branch of a tree against the outside of the window; and, more distinctly, a pair of trembling, veiny hands putting something smooth and cold and round into her own. The smooth cold roundness was accounted for afterwards. The old gentleman, it appeared, had given her a china mug which had been his sister's in her nursery days. It had stood on the mantelpiece at the end house for years, a beautiful old piece with a design of heavy green foliage on a ground of translucent whiteness. Afterwards it got broken, which was strange in that careful home; but Laura carried the design in her mind's eye for the rest of her life and would sometimes wonder if it accounted for her lifelong love of green and white in conjunction. . . .

Around the hamlet cottages played many little children, too young to go to school. Every morning they were bundled into a piece of old shawl crossed on the chest and tied in a hard knot at the back, a slice of food was thrust into their hands and they were told to 'go play' while their mothers got on with the housework. In winter, their little limbs purple-mottled with cold, they would stamp around playing horses or engines. In summer they would make mud pies in the dust, moistening them from their own most intimate water supply. If they fell down or hurt themselves in any other way, they did not run indoors for comfort, for they knew that all they would get would be 'Sarves ye right. You should've looked where you wer' a-goin'!'

They were like little foals turned out to grass, and received about as much attention. They might, and often did, have running noses and chilblains on hands, feet and ear-tips; but they hardly ever were ill enough to have to stay indoors, and grew sturdy and strong, so the system must have suited them. 'Makes 'em hardy,' their mothers said, and hardy, indeed, they became, just as the men and women and older boys and girls of the hamlet were hardy, in body and spirit.

Sometimes Laura and Edmund would go out to play with the other children. Their father did not like this; he said they were little savages already. But their mother maintained that, as they would have to go to school soon, it was better for them to fall in at once with the hamlet ways. 'Besides,' she would say, 'why shouldn't they? There's nothing the matter with Lark Rise folks but poverty, and that's no crime. If it was, we should likely be hung ourselves.'

So the children went out to play and often had happy times, outlining houses with scraps of broken crockery and furnishing them with moss and stones; or lying on their stomachs in the dust to peer down into the deep cracks dry weather always produced in that stiff, clayey soil; or making snow men or sliding on puddles in winter.

Other times were not so pleasant, for a quarrel would arise and kicks and blows would fly freely, and how hard those little two-year-old fists could hit out! To say that a child was as broad as it was long was considered a compliment by the hamlet mothers, and some of those toddlers in their knotted woollen wrappings were as near square as anything human can be. One little girl named Rosie Phillips fascinated Laura. She was plump and hard and as rosy-cheeked as an apple, with the deepest of dimples and hair like bronze wire. No matter how hard the other children bumped into her in the games, she stood four-square, as firm as a little rock. She was a very hard hitter and had little, pointed, white teeth that bit. The two tamer children always came out worst in these conflicts. Then they would make a dash on their long stalky legs for their own garden gate, followed by stones and cries of 'Long-shanks! Cowardy, cowardy custards!'

During those early years at the end house plans were always being made and discussed. Edmund must be apprenticed to a good trade – a carpenter's, perhaps – for if a man had a good trade in his hands he was always sure of a living. Laura might become a school-teacher, or, if that proved impossible, a children's nurse in a good family. But, first and foremost, the family must move from Lark Rise to a house in the market town. It had always been the parents' intention to leave. When he met and married his wife the father was a stranger in the neighbourhood, working for a few months on the restoration of the church in a neighbouring parish and the end house had been taken as a temporary home. Then the children had come and other things had happened to delay the removal. They could not give notice until Michaelmas Day, or another baby was coming, or they must wait until the pig was killed or the allotment crops were brought in; there was always some obstacle, and at the end of seven years they were still at the end house and still talking almost daily about leaving it. Fifty years later the father had died there and the mother was living there alone.

When Laura approached school-going age the discussions became more urgent. Her father did not want the children to go to school with the hamlet children and for once her mother agreed with him. Not because, as he said, they ought to have a better education than they could get at Lark Rise; but because she feared they would tear their clothes and catch cold and get dirty heads going the mile and a half to and from the school in the mother village.

So vacant cottages in the market town were inspected and often it seemed that the next week or the next month they would be leaving Lark Rise for ever; but, again, each time something would happen to prevent the removal, and, gradually, a new idea arose. To gain time, their father would teach the two eldest children to read and write, so that, if approached by the School Attendance Office, their mother could say they were leaving the hamlet shortly and, in the meantime, were being taught at home.

So their father brought home two copies of Mavor's First Reader and taught them the alphabet; but just as Laura was beginning on words of one syllable, he was sent away to work on a distant job, only coming home at week-ends. Laura, left at the 'C-a-t s-i-t-s on the m-a-t' stage, had then to carry her book round after her mother as she went about her housework, asking: 'Please, Mother, what does h-o-u-s-e spell?' or 'W-a-l-k, Mother, what is that?' Often when her mother was too busy or too irritated to

attend to her, she would sit and gaze on a page that might as well have been printed in Hebrew for all she could make of it, frowning and poring over the print as though she would wring out the meaning by force of concentration.

After weeks of this, there came a day when, quite suddenly, as it seemed to her, the printed characters took on a meaning. There were still many words, even in the first pages of that simple primer, she could not decipher; but she could skip those and yet make sense of the whole. 'I'm reading! I'm reading!' she cried aloud. 'Oh, Mother! Oh, Edmund! I'm reading!'

There were not many books in the house, although in this respect the family was better off than its neighbours; for, in addition to 'Father's books', mostly unreadable as yet, and Mother's Bible and *Pilgrim's Progress*, there were a few children's books which the Johnstones had turned out from their nursery when they left the neighbourhood. So, in time, she was able to read Grimms' *Fairy Tales, Gulliver's Travels, The Daisy*

Chain, and Mrs Molesworth's *Cuckoo Clock* and *Carrots*.

As she was seldom seen without an open book in her hand, it was not long before the neighbours knew she could read. They did not approve of this at all. None of their children had learned to read before they went to school, and then only under compulsion, and they thought that Laura, by doing so, had stolen a march on them. So they attacked her mother about it, her father conveniently being away. 'He'd no business to teach the child himself,' they said. 'Schools be the places for teaching, and you'll likely get wrong for him doing it when governess finds out.' Others, more kindly disposed, said Laura was trying her eyes and begged her mother to put an end to her studies; but, as fast as one book was hidden away from her, she found another, for anything in print drew her eyes as a magnet drew steel.

Edmund did not learn to read quite so early; but when he did, he learned more

thoroughly. No skipping unknown words for him and guessing what they meant by the context; he mastered every page before he turned over, and his mother was more patient with his inquiries, for Edmund was her darling.

If the two children could have gone on as they were doing, and have had access to suitable books as they advanced, they would probably have learnt more than they did during their brief schooldays. But that happy time of discovery did not last. A woman, the frequent absences from school of whose child had brought the dreaded Attendance Officer to her door, informed him of the end-house scandal, and he went there and threatened Laura's mother with all manner of penalties if Laura was not in school at nine o'clock the next Monday morning.

So there was to be no Oxford or Cambridge for Edmund. No school other than the National School for either. They would have to pick up what learning they could like chickens pecking for grain – a little at school, more from books, and some by dipping into the store of others. . . .

There were no bought pleasures, and, if there had been, there was no money to pay for them; but there were the sights, sounds and scents of the different seasons: spring with its fields of young wheat-blades bending in the wind as the cloud-shadows swept over them; summer with its ripening grain and its flowers and fruit and its thunder-storms, and how the thunder growled and rattled over that flat land and what boiling, sizzling downpours it brought! With August came the harvest and the fields settled down to the long winter rest, when the snow was often piled high and frozen, so that the buried hedges could be walked over, and strange birds came for crumbs to the cottage doors and hares in search of food left their spoor round the pigsties. . . .

From the time the two children began school they were merged in the hamlet life, sharing the work and play and mischief of their younger companions and taking harsh or kind words from their elders according to circumstances. Yet, although they shared in the pleasures, limitations, and hardships of the hamlet, some peculiarity of mental outlook prevented them from accepting everything that existed or happened there as a matter of course, as the other children did. Small things which passed unnoticed by others interested, delighted, or saddened them. Nothing that took place around them went unnoted; words spoken and forgotten the next moment by the speaker were recorded in their memories, and the actions and reactions of others were impressed on their minds, until a clear, indelible impression of their little world remained with them for life.

Their own lives were to carry them far from the hamlet. Edmund's to South Africa, India, Canada, and, lastly, to his soldier's grave in Belgium. Their credentials presented, they will only appear in this book as observers of and commentators upon the country scene of their birth and early years.

— II —
MEN AFIELD AND AT REST

A MILE and a half up the straight, narrow road in the opposite direction to that of the turnpike, round a corner, just out of sight of the hamlet, lay the mother village of Fordlow. Here, again, as soon as the turning of the road was passed, the scene changed, and the large open fields gave place to meadows and elm trees and tiny trickling streams.

The village was a little, lost, lonely place, much smaller than the hamlet, without a shop, an inn, or a post office, and six miles from a railway station. The little squat church, without spire or tower, crouched back in a tiny churchyard that centuries of use had raised many feet above the road, and the whole was surrounded by tall, windy elms in which a colony of rooks kept up a perpetual cawing. Next came the Rectory, so buried in orchards and shrubberies that only the chimney stacks were visible from the road; then the old tudor farmhouse with its stone, mullioned windows and reputed dungeon. These, with the school and about a dozen cottages occupied by the shepherd, carter, blacksmith, and a few other superior farm-workers, made up the village. Even these few buildings were strung out along the roadside, so far between and so sunken in greenery that there seemed no village at all. It was a standing joke in the hamlet that a stranger had once asked the way to Fordlow after he had walked right through it. The hamlet laughed at the village as 'stuck up'; while the village looked down on 'that gipsy lot' at the hamlet.

Excepting the two or three men who frequented the inn in the evening, the villagers seldom visited the hamlet, which to them represented the outer wilds, beyond the bounds of civilization. The hamlet people, on the other hand, knew the road between the two places by heart, for the church and the school and the farmhouse which was the men's working headquarters were all in the village. The hamlet had only the inn.

Very early in the morning, before daybreak for the greater part of the year, the hamlet men would throw on their clothes, breakfast on bread and lard, snatch the

dinner-baskets which had been packed for them overnight, and hurry off across fields and over stiles to the farm. Getting the boys off was a more difficult matter. Mothers would have to call and shake and sometimes pull boys of eleven or twelve out of their warm beds on a winter morning. Then boots which had been drying inside the fender all night and had become shrunk and hard as boards in the process would have to be coaxed on over chilblains. Sometimes a very small boy would cry over this and his mother to cheer him would remind him that they were only boots, not breeches. 'Good thing you didn't live when breeches wer' made o' leather,' she would say, and tell him about the boy of a previous generation whose leather breeches were so baked up in drying that it took him an hour to get into them. 'Patience! Have patience, my son', his mother had exhorted. 'Remember Job.' 'Job!' scoffed the boy. 'What did he know about patience? He didn't have to wear no leather breeches.'

Leather breeches had disappeared in the 'eighties and were only remembered in telling that story. The carter, shepherd, and a few of the older labourers still wore the traditional smock-frock topped by a round black felt hat, like those formerly worn by clergymen. But this old country style of dress was already out of date; most of the men wore suits of stiff, dark brown corduroy, or, in summer, corduroy trousers and an unbleached drill jacket known as a 'sloppy'.

Most of the young and those in the prime of life were thickset, red-faced men of good medium height and enormous strength who prided themselves on the weights they could carry and boasted of never having had 'an e-ache nor a pa-in' in their lives. The elders stooped, had gnarled and swollen hands and walked badly, for they felt the effects of a life spent out of doors in all weathers and of the rheumatism which tried most of them. These elders wore a fringe of grey whisker beneath the jaw, extending from ear to ear. The younger men sported drooping walrus moustaches. One or two, in advance of the fashion of their day, were clean-shaven; but as Sunday was the only shaving day, the effect of either style became blurred by the end of the week.

They still spoke the dialect, in which the vowels were not only broadened, but in many words doubled. 'Boy' was 'boo-oy', 'coal', 'coo-al', 'pail', 'pay-ull', and so on. In other words, syllables were slurred, and words were run together, as 'brenbu'er' for bread and butter. They had hundreds of proverbs and sayings and their talk was stiff with simile. Nothing was simply hot, cold, or coloured; it was 'as hot as hell'; 'as cold as ice', 'as green as grass', or 'as yellow as a guinea'. A botched-up job done with insufficient materials was 'like Dick's hat-band that went half-way round and tucked'; to try to persuade or encourage one who did not respond was 'putting a poultice on wooden leg'. To be nervy was to be 'like a cat on hot bricks'; to be angry, 'mad as a bull';

or any one might be 'poor as a rat', 'sick as a dog', 'hoarse as a crow', 'as ugly as sin', 'full of the milk of human kindness', or 'stinking with pride'. A temperamental person was said to be 'one o' them as is either up on the roof or down the well'. The dialect was heard at its best on the lips of the few middle-aged men, who had good natural voices, plenty of sense, and a grave, dignified delivery.

The men's incomes were the same to a penny; their circumstances, pleasures, and their daily work were shared in common; but in themselves they differed, as other men of their day differed, in country and town. Some were intelligent, others slow at the uptake; some were kind and helpful, others selfish, some vivacious, others taciturn. If a stranger had gone there looking for the conventional Hodge, he would not have found him.

Nor would he have found the dry humour of the Scottish peasant, or the racy wit and

wisdom of Thomas Hardy's Wessex. These men's minds were cast in a heavier mould and moved more slowly. Yet there were occasional gleams of quiet fun. One man who had found Edmund crying because his magpie, let out for her daily exercise, had not returned to her wicker cage, said: 'Doo'nt 'ee take on like that, my man. You goo an' tell Mrs Andrews about it [naming the village gossip] an' you'll hear where your Maggie's been seen, if 'tis as far away as Stratton.'

Their favourite virtue was endurance. Not to flinch from pain or hardship was their ideal. A man would say, 'He says, says he, that field o' oo-ats's got to come in afore night, for there's a rain a-comin'. But we didn't flinch, not we! Got the last loo-ad under cover by midnight. A'moost too fagged-out to walk home; but we didn't flinch. We done it!' Or, 'Ole bull he comes for me, wi's head down.But I didn't flinch. I ripped off a bit o' loose rail an' went for he. 'Twas him as did th' flinchin'. He! he!' Or a woman would say, 'I set up wi' my poor old mother six nights runnin'; never had me

36

clothes off. But I didn't flinch, an' I pulled her through, for she didn't flinch neither.' Or a young wife would say to the midwife after her first confinement, 'I didn't flinch, did I? Oh, I do hope I didn't flinch.'

The farm was large, extending far beyond the parish boundaries; being, in fact, several farms, formerly in separate occupancy, but now thrown into one and ruled over by the rich old man at the Tudor farmhouse. The meadows around the farmstead sufficed for the carthorses' grazing and to support the store cattle and a couple of milking cows which supplied the farmer's family and those of a few of his immediate neighbours with butter and milk. A few fields were sown with grass seed for hay, and sainfoin and rye were grown and cut green for cattle food. The rest was arable land producing corn and root crops, chiefly wheat.

Around the farmhouse were grouped the farm buildings; stables for the great stamping shaggy-fetlocked carthorses; barns with doors so wide and high that a load of hay could be driven through; sheds for the yellow-and-blue painted farm wagons, granaries with outdoor staircases; and sheds for storing oilcake, artificial manures, and agricultural implements. In the rickyard, tall, pointed, elaborately thatched ricks stood on stone straddles; the dairy indoors, though small, was a model one; there was a profusion of all that was necessary or desirable for good farming.

Labour, too, was lavishly used. Boys leaving school were taken on at the farm as a matter of course, and no time-expired soldier or settler on marriage was ever refused a job. As the farmer said, he could always do with an extra hand, for labour was cheap and the land was well tilled up to the last inch. . . .

With 'Gee!' and 'Wert up!' and 'Who-a-a, now!' the teams would draw out. The boys were hoisted to the backs of the tall carthorses, and the men, walking alongside, filled their clay pipes with shag and drew the first precious puffs of the day, as with cracking of whips, clopping of hooves and jingling of harness, the teams went tramping along the muddy byways.

The field names gave the clue to the fields' history. Near the farmhouse, 'Moat Piece', 'Fishponds', 'Duffus [i.e. dovehouse] Piece', 'Kennels', and 'Warren Piece' spoke of a time before the Tudor house took the place of another and older establishment. Farther on, 'Lark Hill', 'Cuckoos' Clump', 'The Osiers', and 'Pond Piece' were named after natural features, while 'Gibbard's Piece' and 'Blackwell's' probably commemorated otherwise long-forgotten former occupants. The large new fields round the hamlet had been cut too late to be named and were known as 'The Hundred Acres', 'The Sixty Acres', and so on according to their acreage. One or two of the ancients persisted in calling one of these 'The Heath' and

another 'The Racecourse'.

One name was as good as another to most of the men; to them it was just a name and meant nothing. What mattered to them about the fields in which they happened to be working was whether the road was good or bad which led from the farm to it; or if it was comparatively sheltered or one of those bleak open places which the wind hurtled through, driving the rain through the clothes to the very pores; and was the soil easily workable or of back-breaking heaviness or so bound together with that 'hemmed' twitch that a ploughshare could scarcely get through it.

There were usually three or four ploughs to a field, each of them drawn by a team of three horses, with a boy at the head of the leader and the ploughman behind at the shafts. All day, up and down they would go, ribbing the pale stubble with stripes of dark furrows, which, as the day advanced, would get wider and nearer together, until, at length, the whole field lay a rich velvety plum-colour.

Each plough had its following of rooks, searching the clods with sidelong glances for worms and grubs. Little hedgerow birds flitted hither and thither, intent upon getting their tiny share of whatever was going. Sheep, penned in a neighbouring field, bleated complainingly; and above the ma-a-ing and cawing and twittering rose the immemorial cries of the landworker: 'Wert up!' 'Who-o-o-a!'; 'Go it, Poppet!' 'Go it, Lightfoot!' 'Boo-oy, be you deaf, or be you hard of hearin', dang ye!'

After the plough had done its part, the horse-drawn roller was used to break down the clods; then the harrow to comb out and leave in neat piles the weeds and the twitch grass which infested those fields, to be fired later and fill the air with the light blue haze and the scent that can haunt for a lifetime. Then seed was sown, crops were thinned out and hoed and, in time, mown, and the whole process began again.

Machinery was just coming into use on the land. Every autumn appeared a pair of large traction engines, which, posted one on each side of a field, drew a plough across and across by means of a cable. These toured the district under their own steam for hire on the different farms, and the outfit included a small caravan, known as 'the box', for the two drivers to live and sleep in. . . .

Such machinery as the farmer owned was horse-drawn and was only in partial use. In some fields a horse-drawn drill would sow the seed in rows, in others a human sower would walk up and down with a basket suspended from his neck and fling the seed with both hands broadcast. In harvest time the mechanical reaper was already a familiar sight, but it only did a small part of the work; men were still mowing with scythes and a few women were still reaping with sickles. A thrashing machine on hire went from farm to farm and its use was more general; but men at home still thrashed out their allotment crops and their wives' leazings with a flail and winnowed the corn by pouring from sieve to sieve in the wind. . . .

While the ploughmen were in charge of the teams, other men went singly, or in twos or threes, to hoe, harrow, or spread manure in other fields; others cleared ditches and saw to drains, or sawed wood or cut chaff or did other odd jobs about the farmstead. Two or three highly skilled middle-aged men were sometimes put upon piecework, hedging and ditching, sheep-shearing, thatching, or mowing, according to the season. The carter, shepherd, stockman, and blacksmith had each his own specialized job. Important men, these, with two shillings a week extra on their wages and a cottage rent free near the farmstead. . . .

Sometimes afield, instead of the friendly shout, a low hissing whistle would pass between the ploughs. It was a warning note that meant that 'Old Monday', the farm bailiff, had been sighted. He would come riding across the furrows on his little long-tailed grey pony, himself so tall and his steed so dumpy that his feet almost touched the ground, a rosy, shrivelled, nut-cracker-faced old fellow, swishing his ash stick and shouting, 'Hi, men! Ho, men! What do you reckon you're doing!'

He questioned them sharply and found fault here and there, but was in the main fairly just in his dealings with them. He had one great fault in their eyes, however; he was always in a hurry himself and he tried to hurry them, and that was a thing they detested.

The nickname of 'Old Monday', or 'Old Monday Morning', had been bestowed upon him years before when some hitch had occurred and he was said to have cried: 'Ten o'clock Monday morning! Today's Monday, tomorrow's Tuesday, next day's Wednesday – half the week gone and nothing done!' This name, of course, was reserved for his absence; while he was with them it was 'Yes, Muster Morris' and 'No, Muster Morris,' and 'I'll see what I can do, Muster Morris'. A few of the tamer-spirited even called him 'sir'. Then, as soon as his back was turned, some wag would point to it with one hand and slap his own buttocks with the other, saying, but not too loudly, 'My elbow to you, you ole devil!'

At twelve by the sun, or by signal from the possessor of one of the old turnip-faced watches which descended from father to son, the teams would knock off for the dinner-hour. Horses were unyoked, led to the shelter of a hedge or a rick and given their nose-bags, and men and boys threw themselves down on sacks spread out beside them and tin bottles of cold tea were uncorked and red handkerchiefs of food unwrapped. The lucky ones had bread and cold bacon, perhaps the top or the bottom of a cottage loaf, on which the small cube of bacon was placed, with a finger of bread on top, called the thumbpiece, to keep the meat untouched by hand and in position for manipulation with a clasp-knife. The consumption of this food was managed neatly and decently, a small sliver of bacon and a chunk of bread being cut and conveyed to the mouth in one movement. The less fortunate ones munched their bread and lard or morsel of cheese; and the boys with their ends of cold pudding were jokingly bidden not to get 'that 'ere treacle' in their ears.

The food soon vanished, the crumbs from the red handkerchiefs were shaken out for the birds, the men lighted their pipes and the boys wandered off with their catapults down the hedgerows. Often the elders would sit out their hour of leisure discussing

politics, the latest murder story, or local affairs; but at other times, especially when one man noted for that kind of thing was present, they would while away the time in repeating what the women spoke of with shamed voices as 'men's tales'. . . .

A few women still did field work, not with the men, or even in the same field as a rule, but at their own special tasks, weeding and hoeing, picking up stones, and topping and tailing turnips and mangel; or, in wet weather, mending sacks in a barn. Formerly, it was said, there had been a large gang of field women, lawless, slatternly creatures, some of whom had thought nothing of having four or five children out of wedlock. Their day was over; but the reputation they had left behind them had given most country-women a distaste for 'goin' afield'. In the 'eighties about half a dozen of the hamlet women did field work, most of them being respectable middle-aged women who, having got their families off hand, had spare time, a liking for an open-air life, and a longing for a few shillings a week they could call their own.

Their hours, arranged that they might do their housework before they left home in the morning and cook their husband's meal after they returned, were from ten to four, with an hour off for dinner. Their wage was four shillings a week. They worked in sunbonnets, hobnailed boots and men's coats, with coarse aprons of sacking enveloping the lower part of their bodies. One, a Mrs Spicer, was a pioneer in the wearing of trousers; she sported a pair of her husband's corduroys. The others compromised with ends of old trouser legs worn as gaiters. Strong, healthy, weather-beaten, hard as nails, they worked through all but the very worst weathers and declared they would go 'stark, staring mad' if they had to be shut up in a house all day. . . .

On Friday evening, when work was done, the men trooped up to the farmhouse for their wages. These were handed out of a window to them by the farmer himself and acknowledged by a rustic scraping of feet and pulling of forelocks. The farmer had grown too old and too stout to ride horseback, and, although he still made the circuit of his land in his high dogcart every day, he had to keep to the roads, and pay-day was the only time he saw many of his men. Then, if there was cause for complaint, was the time they heard of it. . . .

There is something exhilarating about pay-day, even when the pay is poor and already mortgaged for necessities. With that morsel of gold in their pockets, the men stepped out more briskly and their voices were cheerier than ordinary. When they reached home they handed the half-sovereign straight over to their wives, who gave them back a shilling for the next week's pocket-money. That was the custom of the countryside. The men worked for the money and the women had the spending of it. The men had the best of the bargain. They earned their half-sovereign by hard toil, it is true, but in the open air, at work they liked and took an interest in, and in congenial company. The women, kept close at home, with cooking, cleaning, washing, and mending to do, plus their constant pregnancies and a tribe of children to look after, had also the worry of ways and means on an insufficient income.

Many husbands boasted that they never asked their wives what they did with the money. As long as there was food enough, clothes to cover everybody, and a roof over their heads, they were satisfied, they said, and they seemed to make a virtue of this and think what generous, trusting, fine-hearted fellows they were. If a wife got in debt or complained, she was told: 'You must larn to cut your coat accordin' to your cloth, my gal.' The coats not only needed expert cutting, but should have been made of elastic.

On light evenings, after their tea-supper, the men worked for an hour or two in their gardens or on the allotments. They were first-class gardeners and it was their pride to have the earliest and best of the different kinds of vegetables. They were helped in this by good soil and plenty of manure from their pigsties; but good tilling also played its part. They considered keeping the soil constantly stirred about the roots of growing things the secret of success and used the Dutch hoe a good deal for this purpose. The

process was called 'tickling'. 'Tickle up old Mother Earth and make her bear!' they would shout to each other across the plots, or salute a busy neighbour in passing with: 'Just tickling her up a bit, Jack?'

The energy they brought to their gardening after a hard day's work in the fields was marvellous. They grudged no effort and seemed never to tire. Often, on moonlight nights in spring, the solitary fork of some one who had not been able to tear himself away would be heard and the scent of his twitch fire smoke would float in at the windows. It was pleasant, too, in summer twilight, perhaps in hot weather when water was scarce, to hear the *swish* of water on parched earth in a garden – water which had been fetched from the brook a quarter of a mile distant. 'It's no good stintin' th' land,' they would say. 'If you wants anything out you've got to put summat in, if 'tis only elbow-grease.'

The allotment plots were divided into two, and one half planted with potatoes and the other half with wheat or barley. The garden was reserved for green vegetables, currant and gooseberry bushes, and a few old-fashioned flowers. Proud as they were of their celery, peas and beans, cauliflowers and marrows, and fine as were the specimens they could show of these, their potatoes were their special care, for they had to grow enough to last the year round. They grew all the old-fashioned varieties – ashleaf kidney, early rose, American rose, magnum bonum, and the huge misshaped white elephant. Everybody knew the elephant was an unsatisfactory potato, that it was awkward to handle when paring, and that it boiled down to a white pulp in cooking; but it produced tubers of such astonishing size that none of the men could resist the temptation to plant it. Every year specimens were taken to the inn to be weighed on the only pair of scales in the hamlet, then handed round for guesses to be made of the weight. As the men said, when a patch of elephants was dug up and spread out, 'You'd got summat to put in your eye and look at.'

Very little money was spent on seed; there was little to spend, and they depended mainly upon the seed saved from the previous year. Sometimes, to secure the advantage of fresh soil, they would exchange a bag of seed potatoes with friends living at a distance, and sometimes a gardener at one of the big houses around would give one of them a few tubers of a new variety. These would be carefully planted and tended, and, when the crop was dug up, specimens would be presented to neighbours.

Most of the men sang or whistled as they dug or hoed. There was a good deal of outdoor singing in those days. Workmen sang at their jobs; men with horses and carts sang on the road; the baker, the miller's man, and the fish-hawker sang as they went from door to door; even the doctor and parson on their rounds hummed a tune between their teeth. People were poorer and had not the comforts, amusements, or

knowledge we have today; but they were happier. Which seems to suggest that happiness depends more upon the state of mind – and body, perhaps – than upon circumstances and events.

Fordlow might boast of its church, its school, its annual concert, and its quarterly penny reading, but the hamlet did not envy it these amenities, for it had its own social centre, warmer, more human, and altogether preferable, in the taproom of the 'Wagon and Horses'.

There the adult male population gathered every evening, to sip its half-pints, drop by drop, to make them last, and to discuss local events, wrangle over politics or farming methods, or to sing a few songs 'to oblige'.

It was an innocent gathering. None of them got drunk; they had not money enough, even with beer, and good beer, at two-pence a pint. Yet the parson preached from the pulpit against it, going so far on one occasion as to call it a den of iniquity. ''Tis a great pity he can't come an' see what it's like for his own self,' said one of the older men on the way home from church. 'Pity he can't mind his own business,' retorted a younger one. While one of the ancients put in pacifically, 'Well, 'tis his business, come to think on't. The man's paid to preach, an' he's got to find summat to preach against, stands to reason.'

Only about half a dozen men held aloof from the circle and those were either known to 'have religion', or suspected of being 'close wi' their ha'pence'. . . .

Politics was a favourite topic, for, under the recently extended franchise, every householder was a voter, and they took their new responsibility seriously. A mild Liberalism prevailed, a Liberalism that would be regarded as hide-bound Toryism now, but was daring enough in those days. One man who had been to work in North-ampton proclaimed himself a Radical; but he was cancelled out by the landlord, who called himself a 'true blue'. With the collaboration of this Left and Right, questions of the moment were thrashed out and settled to the satisfaction of the majority.

'Three Acres and a Cow', 'The Secret Ballot', 'The Parnell Commission and Crime', 'Disestablishment of the Church', were catchwords that flew about freely. Sometimes a speech by Gladstone or some other leader would be read aloud from a newspaper and punctuated by the fervent 'Hear! Hear!' of the company. Or Sam, the man with advanced opinions, would relate with reverent pride the story of his meeting and shaking hands with Joseph Arch, the farm-worker's champion. 'Joseph Arch!' he would cry. 'Joseph Arch is the man for the farm labourer!' and knock on the table and wave aloft his pewter mug, very carefully, for every drop was precious.

Then the landlord, standing back to the fireplace with legs astride, would say with the authority of one in his own house, 'It's no good you chaps think'n you're goin' against the gentry. They've got the land and they've got the money, *an'* they'll keep it. Where'd *you* be without them to give you work an' pay your wages, I'd like to know?' and this, as yet, unanswerable question would cast a chill over the company until some one conjured it away with the name of Gladstone. Gladstone! The Grand Old Man! The People's William! Their faith in his power was touching, and all voices would join in singing:

> *God bless the people's William,*
> *Long may he lead the van*
> *Of Liberty and Freedom,*
> *God bless the Grand Old Man.*

All times are times of transition; but the eighteen-eighties were so in a special sense, for the world was at the beginning of a new era, the era of machinery and scientific discovery. Values and conditions of life were changing everywhere. Even to simple

country people the change was apparent. The railways had brought distant parts of the country nearer; newspapers were coming into every home; machinery was superseding hand labour, even on the farms to some extent; food bought at shops, much of it from distant countries, was replacing the home-made and home-grown. Horizons were widening; a stranger from a village five miles away was no longer looked upon as 'a furriner'.

But, side by side with these changes, the old country civilization lingered. Traditions and customs which had lasted for centuries did not die out in a moment. State-educated children still played the old country rhyme games; women still went leazing, although the field had been cut by the mechanical reaper; and men and boys still sang the old country ballads and songs, as well as the latest music-hall successes. So, when a few songs were called for at the 'Wagon and Horses', the programme was

apt to be a curious mixture of old and new.

While the talking was going on, the few younger men, 'boy-chaps', as they were called until they were married, would not have taken a great part in it. Had they shown any inclination to do so, they would have been checked, for the age of youthful dominance was still to come; and, as the women used to say, 'The old cocks don't like it when the young cocks begin to crow.' But, when singing began they came into their own, for they represented the novel.

They usually had first innings with such songs of the day as had percolated so far. 'Over the Garden Wall', with its many parodies, 'Tommy, Make Room for Your Uncle', 'Two Lovely Black Eyes', and other 'comic' or 'sentimental' songs of the moment. The most popular of these would have arrived complete with tune from the outer world; others, culled from the penny song-book they most of them carried, would have to have a tune fitted to them by the singer. They had good lusty voices and

bawled them out with spirit. There were no croon-
ers in those days. . . .

But, always, sooner or later, came the cry, 'Let's give the old 'uns a turn. Here you,
Master Price, what about "It was my father's custom and always shall be mine", or
"Lord Lovell stood", or summat of that sort as has stood the testing o' time?' and
Master Price would rise from his corner of the settle, using the stick he called his 'third
leg' to support his bent figure as he sang:

> Lord Lovell stood at his castle gate,
>   Calming his milk-white steed,
> When up came Lady Nancy Bell
>   To wish her lover God-speed.
>
> 'And where are you going, Lord Lovell?' she said.
>   'And where are you going?' said she.
> 'Oh, I'm going away from my Nancy Bell,
>   Away to a far country-tre-tre;
>   Away to a far coun-tre.'

49

'And when will you come back, Lord Lovell?' she said,
  'When will you come back?' said she.
  'Oh, I will come back in a year and a day,
  Back to my Lady Nancy-ce-ce-ce.
  Back to my Lady Nan-cee.'

But Lord Lovell was gone more than his year and a day, much longer, and when he did at last return, the church bells were tolling:

'And who is it dead?' Lord Lovell, he said.
  'And who is it dead,' said he.
And some said, 'Lady Nancy Bell,'
  And some said, 'Lady Nancy-ce-ce-ce,
  And some said, 'Lady Nan-cee.'

Lady Nancy died as it were to-day;
  And Lord Lovell, he died to-morrow,
And she, she died for pure, pure grief,
  And he, he died for sorrow.

And they buried her in the chancel high,
  And they buried him in the choir;
And out of her grave sprung a red, red rose,
  And out of his sprung a briar.

And they grew till they grew to the church roof,
  And then they couldn't grow any higher;
So they twined themselves in a true lovers' knot,
  For all lovers true to admire.

After that they would all look thoughtfully into their mugs. Partly because the old song had saddened them, and partly because by that time the beer was getting low and the one half-pint had to be made to last until closing time. Then some would say, 'What's old Master Tuffrey up to, over in his corner there? Ain't heard him strike up tonight', and there would be calls for old David's

'Outlandish Knight'; not because they wanted particularly to hear it – indeed, they had heard it so often they all knew it by heart – but because, as they said, 'Poor old feller be eighty-three. Let 'un sing while he can.'

So David would have his turn. He only knew the one ballad, and that, he said, his grandfather had sung, and had said that he had heard his own grandfather sing it. Probably a long chain of grandfathers had sung it; but David was fated to be the last of them. It was out of date, even then, and only tolerated on account of his age. It ran:

An outlandish knight, all from the north lands,
    A-wooing came to me,
He said he would take me to the north lands
    And there he would marry me.

'Go, fetch me some of your father's gold
    And some of your mother's fee,
And two of the best nags out of the stable
    Where there stand thirty and three.'

She fetched him some of her father's gold
    And some of her mother's fee,
And two of the best nags out of the stable
    Where there stood thirty and three.

And then she mounted her milk-white steed
    And he the dapple grey,
And they rode until they came to the sea-shore,
    Three hours before it was day.

'Get off, get off thy milk-white steed
　　And deliver it unto me,
For six pretty maids I have drowned here
　　And thou the seventh shall be.

'Take off, take off, thy silken gown,
　　And deliver it unto me,
For I think it is too rich and too good
　　To rot in the salt sea.'

'If I must take off my silken gown,
　　Pray turn thy back to me,
For I think it's not fitting a ruffian like you
　　A naked woman should see.'

He turned his back towards her
　　To view the leaves so green,
And she took hold of his middle so small
　　And tumbled him into the stream.

And he sank high and he sank low
　　Until he came to the side.
'Take hold of my hand, my pretty ladye,
　　And I will make you my bride.'

'Lie there, lie there, you false-hearted man,
　　Lie there instead of me,
For six pretty maids hast thou drowned here
　　And the seventh hath drowned thee.'

So then she mounted the milk-white steed
　　And led the dapple grey,
And she rode till she came to her own father's door,
　　An hour before it was day.

53

As this last song was piped out in the aged voice, women at their cottage doors on summer evenings would say: 'They'll soon be out now. Poor old Dave's just singing his "Outlandish Knight".'

Songs and singers all have gone, and in their places the wireless blares out variety and swing music, or informs the company in cultured tones of what is happening in China or Spain. Children no longer listen outside. There are very few who could listen, for the thirty or forty which throve there in those days have dwindled to about half a dozen, and these, happily, have books, wireless, and a good fire in their own homes. But, to one of an older generation, it seems that a faint echo of those songs must still linger round the inn doorway. The singers were rude and untaught and poor beyond modern imagining; but they deserve to be remembered, for they knew the now lost secret of being happy on little.

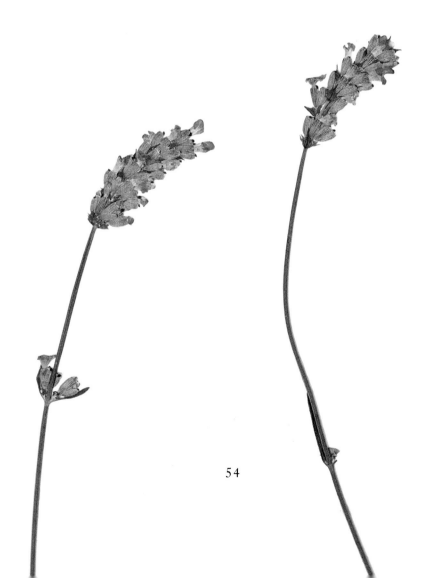

III

SURVIVALS

THERE were three distinct types of home in the hamlet. Those of the old couples in comfortable circumstances, those of the married people with growing families, and the few new homes which had recently been established. The old people who were not in comfortable circumstances had no homes at all worth mentioning, for, as soon as they got past work, they had either to go to the workhouse or find accommodation in the already overcrowded cottages of their children. A father or a mother could usually be squeezed in, but there was never room for both, so one child would take one parent and another the other, and even then, as they used to say, there was always the in-law to be dealt with. It was a common thing to hear ageing people say that they hoped God would be pleased to take them before they got past work and became a trouble to anybody.

But the homes of the more fortunate aged were the most comfortable in the hamlet, and one of the most attractive of these was known as 'Old Sally's'. Never as 'Old Dick's', although Sally's husband, Dick, might have been seen at any hour of the day, digging and hoeing and watering and planting his garden, as much a part of the landscape as his own row of beehives.

He was a little, dry, withered old man, who always wore his smock-frock rolled up round his waist and the trousers on his thin legs gartered with buckled straps. Sally was tall and broad, not fat, but massive, and her large, beamingly good-natured face, with its well-defined moustache and tight, coal-black curls bobbing over each ear, was framed in a white cap frill; for Sally, though still strong and active, was over eighty, and had remained faithful to the fashions of her youth.

She was the dominating partner. If Dick was called upon to decide any question whatever, he would edge nervously aside and say, 'I'll just step indoors and see what Sally thinks about it,' or 'All depends upon what Sally says.' The house was hers and she carried the purse; but Dick was a willing subject and enjoyed her dominion over him. It saved him a lot of thinking, and left him free to give all his time and attention to the growing things in his garden.

Old Sally's was a long, low, thatched cottage with diamond-paned windows winking under the eaves and a rustic porch smothered in honeysuckle. Excepting the inn, it was the largest house in the hamlet, and of the two downstair rooms one was used as a kind of kitchen-storeroom, with pots and pans and a big red crockery water vessel at one end, and potatoes in sacks and peas and beans spread out to dry at the other. The apple crop was stored on racks suspended beneath the ceiling and bunches of herbs dangled below. In one corner stood the big brewing copper in which Sally still brewed with good malt and hops once a quarter. The scent of the last brewing hung over the place till the next and mingled with apple and onion and dried thyme and sage smells, with a dash of soapsuds thrown in, to compound the aroma which remained in the children's

memories for life and caused a whiff of any two of the component parts in any part of the world to be recognized with an appreciative sniff and a mental ejaculation of 'Old Sally's!'

The inner room – 'the house', as it was called – was a perfect snuggery, with walls two feet thick and outside shutters to close at night and a padding of rag rugs, red curtains and feather cushions within. There was a good oak, gate-legged table, a dresser with pewter and willow-pattern plates, and a grandfather's clock that not only told the time, but the day of the week as well. It had even once told the changes of the moon; but the works belonging to that part had stopped and only the fat, full face, painted with eyes, nose and mouth, looked out from the square where the four quarters should have rotated. The clock portion kept such good time that half the hamlet set its own clocks by it. The other half preferred to follow the hooter at the brewery in the market town, which could be heard when the wind was in the right quarter. So there were two times in the hamlet and people would say when asking the hour, 'Is that hooter time, or Old Sally's?'

The garden was a large one, tailing off at the bottom into a little field where Dick grew his corn crop. Nearer the cottage were fruit trees, then the yew hedge, close and solid as a wall, which sheltered the beehives and enclosed the flower garden. Sally had such flowers, and so many of them, and nearly all of them sweet-scented! Wallflowers and tulips, lavender and sweet william, and pinks and old-world roses with enchanting names – Seven Sisters, Maiden's Blush, moss rose, monthly rose, cabbage rose, blood rose, and, most thrilling of all to the children, a big bush of the York and Lancaster rose, in the blooms of which the rival roses mingled in a pied white and red. It seemed as though all the roses in Lark Rise had gathered together in that one garden. Most of the gardens had only one poor starveling bush or none; but, then, nobody else had so much of anything as Sally.

A continual subject for speculation was as to how Dick and Sally managed to live so comfortably with no visible means of support beyond their garden and beehives and the few shillings their two soldier sons might be supposed to send them, and Sally in her black silk on Sundays and Dick never without a few ha'pence for garden seeds or to fill his tobacco pouch. 'Wish they'd tell me how 'tis done,' somebody would grumble. 'I could do wi' a leaf out o' their book.' . . .

Sally could just remember the Rise when it still stood in a wide expanse of open heath, with juniper bushes and furze thickets and close, springly, rabbit-bitten turf. There were only six houses then and they stood in a ring round an open green, all with large gardens and fruit trees and faggot piles. Laura could pick out most of the houses, still in a ring, but lost to sight of each other amongst the newer, meaner dwellings that had sprung up around and between them. Some of the houses had been built on and made into two, others had lost their lean-tos and outbuildings. Only Sally's remained the same, and Sally was eighty. Laura in her lifetime was to see a ploughed field where Sally's stood; but had she been told that she would not have believed it.

Country people had not been so poor when Sally was a girl, or their prospects so hopeless. Sally's father had kept a cow, geese, poultry, pigs, and a donkey-cart to carry his produce to the market town. He could do this because he had commoners' rights and could turn his animals out to graze, and cut furze for firing and even turf to make a lawn for one of his customers. Her mother made butter, for themselves and to sell, baked their own bread, and made candles for lighting. Not much of a light, Sally said, but it cost next to nothing, and, of course, they went to bed early.

Sometimes her father would do a day's work for wages, thatching a rick, cutting and laying a hedge, or helping with the shearing or the harvest. This provided them with ready money for boots and clothes; for food they relied almost entirely on home produce. Tea was a luxury seldom indulged in for it cost five shillings a pound. But country people then had not acquired the taste for tea; they preferred home-brewed.

Everybody worked; the father and mother from daybreak to dark. Sally's job was to mind the cow and drive the geese to the best grass patches. It was strange to picture Sally, a little girl, running with her switch after the great hissing birds on the common, especially as both common and geese had vanished as completely as though they never had been.

Sally had never been to school, for, when she was a child, there was no dame school

near enough for her to attend; but her brother had gone to a night school run by the vicar of an adjoining parish, walking the three miles each way after his day's work was done, and he had taught Sally to spell out a few words in her mother's Bible. After that, she had been left to tread the path of learning alone and had only managed to reach the point where she could write her own name and read the Bible or newspaper by skipping words of more than two syllables. Dick was a little more advanced, for he had had the benefit of the night-school education at first hand. . . .

After Sally's mother died, she became her father's right hand, indoors and out. When the old man became feeble, Dick used to come sometimes to do a bit of hard digging or to farm out the pigsties, and Sally had many tales to tell of the fun they had had carting their bit of hay or hunting for eggs in the loft. When, at a great age, the father died, he left the house and furniture and his seventy-five pounds in the savings bank to Sally, for, by that time, both her brothers were thriving and needed no share.

So Dick and Sally were married and had lived there together for nearly sixty years. It had been a hard, frugal, but happy life. For most of the time Dick had worked as a farm labourer while Sally saw to things about home, for the cow, geese and other stock had long gone the way of the common. But when Dick retired from wage-earning the seventy-five pounds was not only intact, but had been added to. It had been their rule, Sally said, to save something every week, if only a penny or twopence, and the result of their hard work and self-denial was their present comfortable circumstances. 'But us could-n't've done it if us'd gone havin' a great tribe o' children,' Sally would say. 'I didn't never hold wi' havin' a lot o' poor brats and nothin' to put into their bellies. Took us all our time to bring up our two.' She was very bitter about the huge families around her and no doubt would have said more had she been talking to one of maturer age.

They had their little capital reckoned up and allotted: they could manage on so much a year in addition to the earnings of their garden, fowls, and beehives, and that much, and no more, was drawn every year from the bank. 'Reckon it'll about last our time,' they used to say, and it did, although both lived well on into the eighties.

After they had gone, their house stood empty for years. The population of the hamlet was falling and none of the young newly married couples cared for the thatched roof and stone floors. People who lived near used the well; it saved them many a journey. And many were not above taking the railings or the beehive bench or anything made of wood for firing, or gathering the apples or using the poor tattered remnant of the flower garden as a nursery. But nobody wanted to live there.

When Laura visited the hamlet just before the War, the roof had fallen in, the yew hedge had run wild and the flowers were gone, excepting one pink rose which was shedding its petals over the ruin. Today, all has gone, and only the limy whiteness of the soil in a corner of a ploughed field is left to show that a cottage once stood there. . . .

There had been, when Laura was small, one bachelor's establishment near her home. This had belonged to 'the Major', who, as his nickname denoted, had been in the Army. He had served in many lands and then returned to his native place to set up house and do for himself in a neat, orderly, soldier-like manner. All went well until he became old and feeble. Even then, for some years, he struggled on alone in his little home, for he had a small pension. Then he was ill and spent some weeks in Oxford Infirmary. Before he went there, as he had no relatives or special friends, Laura's mother nursed him and helped him to get together the few necessities he had to take with him. She would have visited him at the hospital had it been possible; but money was scarce and her children were too young to be left, so she wrote him a few letters and sent him the newspaper every week. It was, as she said, 'the least anybody could do for the poor old fellow'. But the Major had seen the world and knew its ways and he did not take such small kindnesses as a matter of course.

He came home from the hospital late on Saturday night, after the children were in bed, and, next morning, Laura, waking at early dawn, thought she saw some strange object on her pillow. She dozed and woke again. It was still there. A small wooden box. She sat up in bed and opened it. Inside was a set of doll's dishes with painted wax food upon them – chops and green peas and new potatoes, and a jam tart with criss-cross pastry. Where could it have come from? It was not Christmas or her birthday. Then Edmund awoke and called out he had found an engine. It was a tiny tin engine, perhaps

a penny one, but his delight was unbounded. Then Mother came into their room and said that the Major had brought the presents from Oxford. She had a little red silk handkerchief, such as were worn inside the coat-collar at that time for extra warmth. It was before fur collars were thought of. Father had a pipe and the baby a rattle. It was amazing. To be thought of! To be brought presents, and such presents, by one who was not even a relative! The good, kind Major was in no danger of being forgotten by the family at the end house. Mother made his bed and tidied his room, and Laura was sent with covered plates whenever there was anything special for dinner. She would knock at his door and go in and say in her demure little way, 'Please, Mr Sharman, Mother say could you fancy a little of so-and-so?'

But the Major was too old and ill to be able to live alone much longer, even with such help as the children's mother and other kind neighbours could give. The day came when the doctor called in the relieving officer. The old man was seriously ill; he had no

relatives. There was only one place where he could be properly looked after, and that was the workhouse infirmary. They were right in their decision. He was not able to look after himself; he had no relatives or friends able to undertake the responsibility; the workhouse *was* the best place for him. But they made one terrible mistake. They were dealing with a man of intelligence and spirit, and they treated him as they might have done one in the extreme of senile decay. They did not consult him or tell him what they had decided; but ordered the carrier's cart to call at his house the next morning and wait at a short distance while they, in the doctor's gig, drove up to his door. When they entered, the Major had just dressed and dragged himself to his chair by the fire. 'It's a nice morning, and we've come to take you for a drive,' announced the doctor cheerfully, and, in spite of his protests, they hustled on his coat and had him out and in the carrier's cart in a very few minutes.

Laura saw the carrier touch up his horse with the whip and the cart turn, and she always wished afterwards she had not, for, as soon as he realized where he was being taken, the old soldier, the independent old bachelor, the kind family friend, collapsed and cried like a child. He was beaten. But not for long. Before six weeks were over he was back in the parish and all his troubles were over, for he came in his coffin.

As he had no relatives to be informed, the time appointed for his funeral was not known in the hamlet, or no doubt a few of his old neighbours would have gathered in the churchyard. As it was, Laura, standing back among the graves, a milk-can in her hand, was the only spectator, and that quite by chance. No mourner followed the coffin into the church, and she was far too shy to come forward; but when it was brought out and carried towards the open grave it was no longer unaccompanied, for the clergyman's middle-aged daughter walked behind it, an open prayer-book in her hand and an expression of gentle pity in her eyes. She could barely have known him in life, for he was not a churchgoer; but she had seen the solitary coffin arrive and had hurried across from her home to the church that he might at least have one fellow human being to say 'Farewell' to him. In after years, when Laura heard her spoken of slightingly, and, indeed, often felt irritated herself by her interfering ways, she thought of that graceful action.

The children's grandparents lived in a funny little house out in the fields. It was a round house, tapering off at the top, so there were two rooms downstairs and only one – and that a kind of a loft, with a sloping ceiling – above them. The garden did not adjoin the house, but was shut away between high hedges on the other side of the cart track which led to it. It was full of currant and gooseberry bushes, raspberry canes, and old hardy flowers run wild, almost solid with greenery, for, since the gardener had grown old and stiff in the joints, he had not been able to do much pruning or trimming. There Laura spent many happy hours, supposed to be picking fruit for jam, but for the better part of the time reading or dreaming. One corner, overhung by a damson tree and walled in with bushes and flowers, she called her 'green study'.

Laura's grandfather was a tall old man with snow-white hair and beard and the bluest eyes imaginable. He must at that time have been well on in the seventies, for her mother had been his youngest child and a late-comer. One of her outstanding distinctions in the eyes of her own children was that she had been born an aunt, and, as soon as she could talk, had insisted upon her two nieces, both older than herself, addressing her as 'Aunt Emma'.

Before he retired from active life, the grandfather had followed the old country calling of an eggler, travelling the countryside with a little horse and trap, buying up eggs from farms and cottages and selling them at markets and to shopkeepers. At the back of the round house stood the little lean-to stable in which his pony Dobbin had lived. The children loved to lie in the manger and climb about among the rafters. The death of Dobbin of old age had put an end to his master's eggling, for he had no capital with which to buy another horse. Far from it. Moreover, by that time he was himself suffering from Dobbin's complaint; so he settled down to doing what he could in his garden and making a private daily round on his own feet, from his home to the end house, from the end house to church, and back home again.

At the church he not only attended every service, Sunday and weekday, but, when there was no service, he would go there alone to pray and meditate, for he was a deeply religious man. At one time he had been a local preacher, and had walked miles on

Sunday evenings to conduct, in turn with others, the services at the cottage meeting houses in the different villages. In old age he had returned to the Church of England, not because of any change of opinion, for creeds did not trouble him – his feet were too firmly planted on the Rock upon which they are all founded – but because the parish church was near enough for him to attend its services, was always open for his private devotions, and the music there, poor as it was, was all the music left to him.

Some members of his old meeting-house congregations still remembered what they considered his inspired preaching 'of the Word'. 'You did ought to be a better gal, wi' such a gran'fer,' said a Methodist woman to Laura one day when she saw her crawl through a gap in a hedge and tear her new pinafore. But Laura was not old enough to appreciate her grandfather, for he died when she was ten, and his loving care for her mother, his youngest and dearest child, led to many lectures and reproofs. Had he seen the torn pinafore, it would certainly have provoked both. However, she had just sufficient discrimination to know he was better than most people. . . .

One of Laura's earliest memories was of her grandfather coming through the gate and up the end house garden in his old-fashioned close-fitting black overcoat and bowler hat, his beard nicely trimmed and shining, with a huge vegetable marrow under his arm. He came every morning and seldom came empty-handed. He would bring a little basket of early raspberries or green peas, already shelled, or a tight little bunch of sweet williams and moss rosebuds, or a baby rabbit, which someone else had given him – always something. He would come indoors, and if anything in the house was broken, he would mend it, or he would take a stocking out of his pocket and sit down and knit, and all the time he was working he would talk in a kind, gentle voice to his daughter, calling her 'Emmie'. Sometimes she would cry as she told him of her troubles, and he would get up and smooth her hair and wipe her eyes and say, 'That's better! That's better! Now you're going to be my own brave little wench! And remember, my dear, there's One above who knows what's best for us, though we may not see it ourselves at the time.'

By the middle of the 'eighties the daily visits had ceased, for the chronic rheumatism against which he had fought was getting the better of him. First, the church was too far for him; then the end house; then his own garden across the road; and at last his world narrowed down to the bed

65

upon which he was lying. That bed was not the four-poster with the silk-and-satin patchwork quilt in rich shades of red and brown and orange which stood in the best downstairs bedroom, but the plain white bed beneath the sloping ceiling in the little whitewashed room under the roof. He had slept there for years, leaving his wife the downstairs room, that she might not be disturbed by his fevered tossing during his rheumatic attacks, and also because, like many old people, he woke early, and liked to get up and light the fire and read his Bible before his wife was ready for her cup of tea to be taken to her.

Gradually, his limbs became so locked he could not turn over in bed without help. Giving to and doing for others was over for him. He would lie upon his back for hours, his tired old blue eyes fixed upon the picture nailed on the wall at the foot of his bed. It was the only coloured thing in the room; the rest was bare whiteness. It was of the Crucifixion, and, printed above the crown of thorns were the words:

This have I done for thee.

And underneath the pierced and bleeding feet:

What has thou done for me?

His two years' uncomplaining endurance of excruciating pain answered for him.

When her husband was asleep, or lying, washed and tended, gazing at his picture, Laura's grandmother would sit among her feather cushions downstairs reading *Bow Bells* or the *Princess Novelettes* or the *Family Herald*. Except when engaged in housework, she was never seen without a book in her hand. It was always a novelette, and she had a large assortment of these which she kept tied up in flat parcels, ready to exchange with other novelette readers.

She had been very pretty when she was young. 'The Belle of Hornton', they had called her in her native village, and she often told Laura of the time when her hair had reached down to her knees, like a great yellow cape, she said, which covered her. Another of her favourite stories was of the day when she had danced with a real lord. It was at his coming-of-age celebrations, and a great honour, for he had passed over his own friends and the daughters of his tenants in favour of one who was but a gamekeeper's daughter. Before the evening was over he had whispered in her ear that she was the prettiest girl in the country, and she had cherished the compliment all her life. There were no further developments. My Lord was My Lord, and Hannah Pollard was Hannah Pollard, a poor girl, but the daughter of decent parents. No

further developments were possible in real life, though such affairs ended differently in her novelettes. Perhaps that was why she enjoyed them.

It was difficult for Laura to connect the long, yellow hair and the white frock with blue ribbons worn at the coming-of-age fête with her grandmother, for she saw her only as a thin, frail old woman who wore her grey hair parted like curtains and looped at the ears with little combs. Still, there was something which made her worth looking at. Laura's mother said it was because her features were good. 'My mother,' she would say, 'will look handsome in her coffin. Colour goes and the hair turns grey, but the framework lasts.' . . .

Laura's grandmother had never tramped ten miles on a Sunday night to hear her husband preach in a village chapel. She had gone to church once every Sunday, unless it rained or was too hot, or she had a cold, or some article of her attire was too shabby. She was particular about her clothes and liked to have everything handsome about her. In her bedroom there were pictures and ornaments, as well as the feather cushions and silk patchwork quilt.

When she came to the end house, the best chair was placed by the fire for her and the best possible tea put on the table, and Laura's mother did not whisper her troubles to her as she did to her father. If some little thing did leak out, she would only say, 'All men need a bit of humouring.' Some women, too, thought Laura, for she could see that her grandmother had always been the one to be indulged and spared all trouble and unpleasantness. . . .

After her husband died, she went away to live with her eldest son, and the round house shared the fate of Sally's. Where it stood is now a ploughed field. The husband's sacrifices, the wife's romance, are as though they had never been – 'melted into air, into thin air'. . . .

——— IV ———
CALLERS

CALLERS made a pleasant diversion in the hamlet women's day, and there were more of these than might have been expected. The first to arrive on Monday morning was old Jerry Parish with his cartload of fish and fruit. As he served some of the big houses on his round, Jerry carried quite a large stock; but the only goods he took round to the doors at Lark Rise were a box of bloaters and a basket of small, sour oranges. The bloaters were sold at a penny each and the oranges at three a penny. Even at these prices they were luxuries; but, as it was still only Monday and a few coppers might remain in a few purses, the women felt at liberty to crowd round his cart to examine and criticize his wares, even if they bought nothing.

Two or three of them would be tempted to buy a bloater for their midday meal, but it had to be a soft-roed one, for, in nearly every house there were children under school age at home; so the bloater had to be shared, and the soft roes spread upon bread for the smallest ones.

'Lor' blime me!' Jerry used to say. 'Never knowed such a lot in me life for soft roes. Good job I ain't a soft-roed 'un or I should've got aten up meself before now.' And he pinched the bloaters between his great red fingers, pretended to consider the matter with his head on one side, then declared each separate fish had the softest of soft roes, whether it had or not. 'Oozin', simply oozin' with goodness, I tell ye!' and oozing it certainly was when released from his grip. 'But what's the good of one bloater amongst the lot of ye? Tell ye what I'll do,' he would urge. 'I'll put ye in these three whoppers for tuppence-ha'penny.'

It was no good. The twopence-halfpenny was never forthcoming; even the penny could so ill be spared that the purchaser often felt selfish and greedy after she had parted with it; but, after a morning at the washtub, she needed a treat so badly, and a bloater made a tasty change from her usually monotonous diet. . . .

Mr Wilkins, the baker, came three times a week. His long, lank figure, girded by a white apron which always seemed about to slip down over his hips, was a familiar one at the end house. He always stayed there for a cup of tea, for which he propped himself up against the end of the dresser. He would never sit down; he said he had not time, and that was why he did not stop to change his flour-dusty bakehouse clothes before he started on his round.

He was no ordinary baker, but a ship's carpenter by trade who had come to the neighbouring village on a visit to relatives, met his present wife, married her, and cast anchor inland. Her father was old, she was the only child, and the family business had to be attended to; so, partly for love and partly for future gain he had given up the sea, but he still remained a sailor at heart.

He would stand in the doorway of Laura's home and look out at the wheatfields billowing in the breeze and the white clouds hurrying over them, and say: 'All very fine; but it seems a bit dead to me, right away from the sea, like this.' And he would tell the children how the waves pile up in a storm, 'like the wall of a house coming down on your ship', and about other seas, calm and bright as a looking-glass, with little islands and palm trees – but treacherous, too – and treacherous little men living in palm leaf huts, 'their faces as brown as your frock, Laura.' Once he had been shipwrecked and spent nine days in an open boat, the last two without water. His tongue had stuck to the roof of his mouth and he had spent weeks in hospital.

'And yet,' he would say, 'I'd dearly love just one more trip; but my dear wife would cry her eyes out if I mentioned it, and the business, of course, couldn't be left. No. I've swallowed the anchor, all right. I've swallowed the anchor.'

Mr Wilkins brought the image of the real living sea to the end house; otherwise the children would have only known it in pictures. True, their mother in her nursing days had been to the seaside with her charges and had many pleasant stories to tell of walks on piers, digging on sands, gathering seaweed, and shrimping with nets. But the seaside was different – delightful in its way, no doubt, but nothing like the wide tumbling ocean with ships on it. . . .

Many casual callers passed through the hamlet. Travelling tinkers with their barrows, braziers, and twirling grindstones turned aside from the main road and came singing:

> *Any razors or scissors to grind?*
> *Or anything else in the tinker's line?*
> *Any old pots or kettles to mend?*

After squinting into any leaking vessel against the light, or trying the edges of razors or scissors upon the hard skin of their palms, they would squat by the side of the road to

work, or start their emery wheel whizzing, to the delight of the hamlet children, who always formed a ring around any such operations. . . .

There must have been hundreds of tramps on the roads at that time. It was a common sight, when out for a walk, to see a dirty, unshaven man, his rags topped with a battered bowler, lighting a fire of sticks by the roadside to boil his tea-can. Sometimes he would have a poor bedraggled woman with him and she would be lighting the fire while he lolled at ease on the turf or picked out the best pieces from the bag of food they had collected at their last place of call.

Some of them carried small, worthless things to sell – matches, shoe-laces, or dried-lavender bags. The children's mother often bought from these out of pity; but never from the man who sold oranges, for they had seen him on one of their walks, spitting on his oranges and polishing them with a filthy rag. Then there was the woman

who, very early one morning, knocked at the door with small slabs of tree-bark in her apron. She was cleaner and better dressed than the ordinary tramp and brought with her a strong scent of lavender. The bark appeared to be such as could have been hacked with a clasp-knife from the nearest pine tree; but she claimed for it a very different origin. It was the famous lavender bark, she said, brought from foreign parts by her sailor son. One fragment kept among clothes was not only an everlasting perfume, but it was also death to moths. 'You just smell it, my dears,' she said, handing pieces to the mother and the children, who had crowded to the door.

It certainly smelt strongly of lavender. The children handled it lovingly, fascinated by a substance which had travelled so far and smelt so sweetly.

She asked sixpence a slab; but obligingly came down to two-pence, and three pieces were purchased and placed in a fancy bowl on the side table to perfume the room and to be exhibited as a rarity.

Alas! the vendor had barely time to clear out of the hamlet before all the perfume had evaporated and the bark became what it had been before she sprinkled it with oil of lavender – just ordinary bark from a pine trunk!

Such brilliance was exceptional. Most of the tramps were plain beggars. 'Please could you give me a morsel of bread, for I be so hungry. I'm telling God I haven't put a bite between my lips since yesterday morning' was a regular formula with them when they knocked at the door of a cottage; and, although many of them looked well-nourished, they were never turned away. Thick slices, which could ill be spared, were plastered with lard; the cold potatoes which the housewife had intended to fry for her own dinner were wrapped in newspaper, and by the time they left the hamlet they were insured against starvation for at least a week. The only reward for such generosity, beyond the whining professional 'God bless ye', was the cheering reflection that

however badly off one might be oneself, there were others poorer. . . .

The packman, or pedlar, once a familiar figure in that part of the country, was seldom seen in the 'eighties. People had taken to buying their clothes at the shops in the market town, where fashions were newer and prices lower. But one last survivor of the once numerous clan still visited the hamlet at long and irregular intervals.

He would turn aside from the turnpike and come plodding down the narrow hamlet road, an old white-headed, white-bearded man, still hale and rosy, although almost bent double under the heavy, black canvas-covered pack he carried strapped on his shoulders. 'Anything out of the pack today?' he would ask at each house, and, at the least encouragement, fling down his load and open it on the doorstep. He carried a tempting variety of goods: dress-lengths and shirt-lengths and remnants to make up for the children; aprons and pinafores, plain and fancy; corduroys for the men, and coloured scarves and ribbons for Sunday wear.

'That's a bit of right good stuff, ma'am, that is,' he would say, holding up some dress-length to exhibit it. 'A gown made of this piece'd last anybody for ever and then make 'em a good petticoat afterwards.' Few of the hamlet women could afford to test the quality of his piece goods; cottons or tapes, or a paper of pins, were their usual purchases; but his dress-lengths and other fabrics were of excellent quality and wore much longer than anyone would wish anything to wear in these days of rapidly changing fashions. It was from his pack the soft, warm woollen, grey with a white fleck in it, came to make the frock Laura wore with a little black satin apron and a bunch of snowdrops pinned to the breast when she went to sell stamps in the post office. . . .

The greatest thrill of all and the one longest remembered in the hamlet, was provided by the visit of a cheap-jack about half-way through the decade. One autumn evening, just before dusk, he arrived with his cartload of crockery and tinware and set out his stock on the grass by the roadside before a backcloth painted with icebergs and penguins and polar bears. Soon he had his naphtha lamps flaring and was clashing his basins together like bells and calling: 'Come buy! Come buy!'

It was the first visit of a cheap-jack to the hamlet and there was great excitement. Men, women, and children rushed from the houses and crowded around in the circle of light to listen to his patter and admire his wares. And what bargains he had! The tea-service decorated with fat, full-blown pink roses: twenty-one pieces and not a flaw in any one of them. The Queen had purchased its fellow set for Buckingham Palace it appeared. The teapots, the trays, the nests of dishes and basins, and the set of bedroom china which made everyone blush when he selected the most intimate utensil to rap with his knuckles to show it rang true.

'Two bob!' he shouted. 'Only two bob for this handsome set of jugs. Here's one for your beer and one for your milk and another in case you break one of the other two. Nobody willing to speculate? Then what about this here set of trays, straight from Japan and the peonies hand-painted; or this lot of basins, exact replicas of the one the Princess of Wales supped her gruel from when Prince George was born. Why damme, they cost me more n'r that. I could get twice the price I'm asking in Banbury tomorrow; but I'll give 'em to you, for you can't call it selling, because I like your faces and me load's heavy for me 'oss. Alarming bargains! Tremendous sacrifices! Come buy! Come buy!'

But there were scarcely any offers. A woman here and there would give threepence for a large pudding-basin or sixpence for a tin saucepan. The children's mother bought a penny nutmeg-grater and a set of wooden spoons for cooking; the innkeeper's wife ran to a

dozen tumblers and a ball of string; then there was a long pause during which the vendor kept up a continual stream of jokes and anecdotes which sent his audience into fits of laughter. Once he broke into song:

There was a man in his garden walked
And cut his throat with a lump of chalk;
His wife, she knew not what she did,
She strangled herself with the saucepan lid.
There was a man and a fine young fellow
Who poisoned himself with an umbrella.
Even Joey in his cradle shot himself dead with a silver ladle.
When you hear this horrible tale
It makes your faces all turn pale,
Your eyes go green, you're overcome,
So tweedle, tweedle, tweedle twum.

All very fine entertainment; but it brought him no money and he began to suspect that he would draw a blank at Lark Rise.

'Never let it be said,' he implored, 'that this is the poverty-strickenist place on God's earth. Buy something, if only for your own credit's sake. Here!' snatching up a pile of odd plates, 'Good dinner-plates for you. Every-one a left-over from a first-class service. Buy one of these and you'll have the satisfaction of knowing you're eating off the same ware as lords and dukes. Only three-halfpence each. Who'll buy? Who'll buy?'

There was a scramble for the plates, for nearly every one could muster three-halfpence; but every time anything more costly was produced there was dead silence. Some of the women began to feel uncomfortable. 'Don't be poor and look poor, too' was their motto, and here they were looking poor indeed, for who, with money in their pockets, could have resisted such wonderful bargains.

Then the glorious unexpected happened. The man had brought the pink rose tea-service forward again and was handing one of the cups round. 'You just look at the light through it – and you, ma'am – and you. Ain't it lovely china, thin as an eggshell, practically transparent, and with every one of them roses hand-painted with a brush? You can't let a set like that go out of the place, now can you? I can see all your mouths a-watering. You run home, my dears, and bring out them stockings from under the mattress and the first one to get back shall have it for twelve bob.'

Each woman in turn handled the cup lovingly, then shook her head and passed it on. None of them had stockings of savings hidden away. But, just as the man was receiving back the cup, a little roughly, for he was getting discouraged, a voice spoke up in the background.

'How much did you say, mister? Twelve bob? I'll give you ten.' It was John Price, who, only the night before, had returned from his soldiering in India. A very ordinary sort of chap at most times, for he was a teetotaller and stood no drinks at the inn, as a returned soldier should have done; but now, suddenly, he became important. All eyes were upon him. The credit of the hamlet was at stake.

'I'll give you ten bob.'

'Can't be done, matey. Cost me more nor that. But, look see, tell you what I will do. You give me eleven and six and I'll throw in this handsome silver-gilt vase for your mantelpiece.'

'Done!' The bargain was concluded; the money changed hands, and the reputation of the hamlet was rehabilitated. Willing hands helped John carry the tea-service to his home. Indeed, it was considered an honour to be trusted with a cup. His bride-to-be was still away in service and little knew how many were envying her that night. To have such a lovely service awaiting her return, no cracked or odd pieces, every piece alike and all so lovely; lucky, lucky, Lucy! But though they could not help envying her a little, they shared in her triumph, for surely such a purchase must shed a glow of reflected prosperity on the whole hamlet. Though it might not be convenient to all of them to buy very much on that particular night, the man must see there *was* a bit of money in the place and folks who knew how to spend it.

What came after was anti-climax, and yet very pleasant from the end house children's point of view. A set of pretty little dishes, suitable for holding jam, butter or fruit, according to size, was being exhibited. The price had gone down from half a crown to a shilling without response, when once more a voice spoke up in the background. 'Pass them over, please. I expect my wife can find a use for them,' and, behold, it was the children's father who had halted on his way home from work to see what the lights and the crowd meant.

Perhaps in all the man took a pound that night, which was fifteen shillings more than any one could have foretold; but it was not sufficient to tempt him to come again, and thenceforth the year was dated as 'that time the cheap-jack came'.

A familiar sight at Lark Rise was that of a young girl – any young girl between ten and thirteen – pushing one of the two perambulators in the hamlet round the Rise with a smallish-sized, oak clothes box with black handles lashed to the seat. Those not already informed who met her would read the signs and inquire: 'How is your mother' – or your sister or your aunt – 'getting on?' and she, well-primed, would answer

demurely, 'As well as can be expected under the circumstances, thank you, Mrs So-and-So.'

She had been to the Rectory for THE BOX, which appeared
almost simultaneously with every new baby, and a gruelling
time she would have had pushing her load the mile and a half
and, at the same time, keeping it from slipping from its narrow
perch. But, very soon, such small drawbacks would be forgotten in the pleasure of seeing it unpacked. It contained half a
dozen of everything – tiny shirts, swathes, long flannel barrows, nighties, and napkins, made, kept in repair, and lent for
every confinement by the clergyman's daughter. In addition to the
loaned clothes, it would contain, as a gift, packets of tea and sugar
and a tin of patent groats for making gruel.

The box was a popular institution. Any farm labourer's wife,
whether she attended church or not, was made welcome to the loan of
it. It appeared in most of the cottages at regular intervals and seemed to
the children as much a feature of family life as the new babies. It was so constantly
in demand that it had to have an understudy, known as 'the second-best box',
altogether inferior, which fell to the lot of those careless matrons who had
neglected to bespeak the loan the moment they 'knew their luck again'.

The boxes were supposed to be returned at the end of a month with the clothes
freshly laundered; but, if no one else required them, an extension could be had, and
many mothers were allowed to keep their box until, at six or seven weeks old, the baby
was big enough to be put into short clothes; so saving them the cost of preparing a
layette other than the one set of clothes got ready for the infant's arrival. Even that
might be borrowed. The stock at the end house was several times called for in what, by
a polite fiction, passed as an emergency. Other women had their own baby clothes,
beautifully sewn and laundered; but there was scarcely one who did not require the
clothes in the box to supplement them. For some reason or other, the box was never
allowed to go out until the baby had arrived.

The little garments on loan were all good quality and nicely trimmed with embroidery and hand tucking. The clergyman's daughter also kept two christening robes to
lend to the mothers, and made a new frock, as a gift, for every baby's 'shortening'.
Summer or winter, these little frocks were made of flowered print, blue for the boys
and pink for the girls, and every one of the tiny, strong stitches in them were done by
her own hands. She got little credit for this. The mothers, like the children, looked
upon the small garments, both loaned and given, as a provision of Nature. Indeed, they
were rather inclined to criticize. One woman ripped off the deep flounce of old
Buckinghamshire lace from the second-best christening robe and substituted a frill of

coarse, machine-made embroidery, saying she was not going to take her child to church 'trigged out' in that old-fashioned trash. As she had not troubled to unpick the stitches, the lace was torn beyond repair, and the gown ever after was decidedly second-best, for the best one was the old Rectory family christening robe and made of the finest lawn, tucked and inserted all over with real Valenciennes.

When the hamlet babies arrived, they found good clothes awaiting them, and the best of all nourishment – Nature's own. The mothers did not fare so well. It was the fashion at that time to keep maternity patients on low diet for the first three days, and the hamlet women found no difficulty in following this régime; water gruel, dry toast, and weak tea was their menu. When the time came for more nourishing diet, the parson's daughter made for every patient one large sago pudding, followed up by a jug of veal broth. After these were consumed they returned to their ordinary food, with a half-pint of stout a day for those who could afford it. No milk was taken, and yet their own milk supply was abundant. Once, when a bottle-fed baby was brought on a visit to the hamlet, its bottle was held up as a curiosity. It had a long, thin rubber tube for the baby to suck through which must have been impossible to clean.

The only cash outlay in an ordinary confinement was half a crown, the fee of the old woman who, as she said, saw the beginning and end of everybody. She was, of course, not a certified midwife; but she was a decent, intelligent old body, clean in her person and methods and very kind. For the half-crown she officiated at the birth and came every morning for ten days to bath the baby and make the mother comfortable. She also tried hard to keep the patient in bed for the ten days; but with little success. Some mothers refused to stay there because they knew they were needed downstairs; others because they felt so strong and fit they saw no reason to lie there. Some women actually got up on the third day, and, as far as could be seen at the time, suffered no ill effects.

Complications at birth were rare; but in the two or three cases where they did occur during her practice, old Mrs Quinton had sufficient skill to recognize the symptoms and send post haste for the doctor. No mother lost her life in childbed during the decade. . . .

The general health of the hamlet was excellent. The healthy, open-air life and the abundance of coarse but wholesome food must have been largely responsible for that; but lack of imagination may also have played a part. Such people at that time did not look for or expect illness, and there were not as many patent medicine advertisements then as now to teach them to search for symptoms of minor ailments in themselves. Beecham's and Holloway's Pills were already familiar to all

80

newspaper readers, and a booklet advertising Mother Siegel's Syrup arrived by post at every house once a year. But only Beecham's Pills were patronized, and those only by a few; the majority relied upon an occasional dose of Epsom salts to cure all ills. One old man, then nearly eighty, had for years drunk a teacupful of frothing soap-suds every Sunday morning. 'Them cleans the outers,' he would say, 'an' stands to reason they must clean th' innards, too.' His dose did not appear to do him any harm; but he made no converts.

Although only babies and very small children had baths, the hamlet folks were cleanly in their persons. The women would lock their cottage doors for a whole afternoon once a week to have what they called a 'a good clean up'. This consisted of stripping to the waist and washing downward; then stepping into a footbath and washing upward. 'Well, I feels all the better for that,' some woman would say

complacently. 'I've washed up as far as possible and down as far as possible,' and the ribald would inquire what poor 'possible' had done that that should not be included.

Toothbrushes were not in general use; few could afford to buy such luxuries; but the women took a pride in their strong white teeth and cleaned them with a scrap of clean, wet rag dipped in salt. Some of the men used soot as a tooth-powder.

After a confinement, if the eldest girl was too young and there was no other relative available, the housework, cooking, and washing would be shared among the neighbours, who would be repaid in kind when they themselves were in like case.

Babies, especially young babies, were adored by their parents and loved and petted and often spoilt by the whole family until another arrived; then, as they used to say, its 'nose was put out of joint'; all the adoration was centred on the newcomer and the ex-baby was fortunate if it had a still devoted elder sister to stand by it.

In the production of their large families the parents appeared reckless. One obvious method of birth control, culled from the Old Testament, was known in the hamlet and practised by one couple, which had managed to keep their family down to four. The wife told their secret to another woman, thinking to help her; but it only brought scorn down on her own head. 'Did you ever! Fancy begrudging a little child a bit o' food, the nasty greedy selfish hussy, her!' was the general verdict. But, although they protested so volubly, and bore their own frequent confinements with courage and cheerfulness, they must have sometimes rebelled in secret, for there was great bitterness in the tone in which in another mood they would say: 'The wife ought to have the first child and the husband the second, then there wouldn't ever be any more.'

That showed how the land lay, as Laura's mother said to her in later life. She herself lived to see the decline in the birth-rate, and, when she discussed it with her daughter in the early 1930s, laughed heartily at some of the explanations advanced by the learned, and said: 'If they knew what it meant to carry and bear and bring up a child themselves, they wouldn't expect the women to be in a hurry to have a second or third now they've got a say in the matter. Now, if they made it a bit easier for people, dividing it out a bit, so to speak, by taking over some of the money worry. It's never seemed fair to my mind that the one who's got to go through all a confinement means should have to scrape and pinch beforehand to save a bit as well. Then there's the other child or children. What mother wants to rob those she's already got by bringing in another to share what there's too little of already?'

None of the unmarried hamlet girls had babies in the 'eighties, although there must have been quite a crop of illegitimate births a few years earlier, for when the attendance register was called out at school the eldest children of several families answered to another surname than that borne by their brothers and sisters and by which they themselves were commonly known. These would be the children of couples who had married after the birth of their first child, a common happening at that time and little thought of.

In the 'eighties a young woman of thirty came from Birmingham to have her illegitimate baby at her sister's home in the hamlet, and a widow who had already three legitimate children and afterwards married again managed to produce two children between her two marriages. These births passed without much comment; but when a young girl of sixteen whose home was out in the fields near the hamlet was known to be 'in trouble' public feeling was stirred.

One evening, a few weeks before the birth, Emily passed through the hamlet with her father on their way to interview the young man she had named as responsible for her condition. It was a sad little sight. Emily, who had so recently been romping with the other children, going slowly, unwillingly, and red-eyed from crying, her tell-tale figure enveloped in her mother's plaid shawl, and her respectable, grey-headed father in his Sunday suit urging her to 'Come on!' as though longing to be through with a

disagreeable business. Women came to their cottage gates and children left their play to watch them pass by, for every one knew or guessed their errand, and much sympathy was felt towards them on account of Emily's youth and her parents' respectability.

The interview turned out even more mortifying than the father could have expected, for Emily had named the young son of the house where she had been in service, and he not only repudiated the charge, but was able to prove that he had been away from home for some time before and after the crucial date. Yet, in spite of the evidence, the neighbours still believed Emily's version of the story and treated her as a wronged heroine, to be petted and made much of. Perhaps they made too much of her, for what should have been an episode turned into a habit, and, although she never married, Emily had quite a good-sized family.

The hamlet women's attitude towards the unmarried mother was contradictory. If one of them brought her baby on a visit to the hamlet they all went out of their way to pet and fuss over them. 'The pretty dear!' they would cry. 'How ever can anybody say such a one as him ought not to be born. Ain't he a beauty! Ain't he a size! They always say, you know, that that sort of child is the finest. An' don't you go mindin' what folks says about you, me dear. It's only the good girls, like you, that has 'em; the others is too artful!'

But they did not want their own daughters to have babies before they were married. 'I allus tells my gals,' one woman would say confidentially to another, 'that if they goes getting theirselves into trouble they'll have to go to th' work'us, for I won't have 'em at home.' And the other would agree, saying, 'So I tells mine, an' I allus think that's why I've had no trouble with 'em.'

To those who knew the girls, the pity was that their own mothers should so misjudge their motives for keeping chaste; but there was little room for their finer feelings in the hamlet mother's life. All her strength, invention and understanding were absorbed in caring for her children's bodies; their mental and spiritual qualities were outside her range. At the same time, if one of the girls had got into trouble, as they called it, the mother would almost certainly have had her home and cared for her. There was more than one home in the hamlet where the mother was bringing up a grandchild with her own younger children, the grandchild calling the grandmother 'Mother'.

If, as sometimes happened, a girl had to be married in haste, she was thought none the worse of on that account. She had secured her man. All was well. ''Tis but Nature' was the general verdict.

But though they were lenient with such slips, especially when not in their own families, anything in the way of what they called 'loose living' was detested by them. Only once in the history of the hamlet had a case of adultery been known to the general public, and, although that had occurred ten or twelve years before, it was still talked of in the 'eighties. The guilty couple had been treated to 'rough music'. Effigies of the pair had been made and carried aloft on poles by torchlight to the house of the woman, to the accompaniment of the banging of pots, pans, and coal-shovels, the screeching of tin whistles and mouth-organs, and cat-calls, hoots, and jeers. The man, who was a lodger at the woman's house, disappeared before daybreak the next morning, and soon afterwards the woman and her husband followed him.

About the middle of the decade, the memory of that historic night was revived when an unmarried woman with four illegitimate children moved into a vacant house in the hamlet. Her coming raised a fury of indignation. Words hitherto only heard by the children when the Lessons were read in church were flung about freely: 'harlot' was one of the mildest. The more ardent moralists were for stoning her or driving her out of the place with rough music. The more moderate proposed getting her landlord to turn her out as a bad character. However, upon closer acquaintance, she turned out to be so clean, quiet, and well-spoken, that her sins, which she had apparently abandoned, were forgiven her, and one after another of the neighbours began 'passing the time of day' with her when they met. Then, as though willing to do anything in reason to conform to their standard, she got married to a man who had been navvying on a stretch of new railway line and then settled down to farm labour. So there were wedding bells instead of rough music and the family gradually merged into ordinary hamlet life.

It was the hamlet's gain. One of the boys was musical, an aunt had bought him a good melodeon, and, every light evening, he played it for hours on the youths' gathering round in front of the 'Wagon and Horses'.

Before his arrival there had been no musical instrument of any kind at Lark Rise, and, in those days before gramophones or wireless, any one who liked 'a bit of a tune' had to go to church to hear it, and then it would only be a hymn tune wheezed out by an ancient harmonium. Now they could have all the old favourites – 'Home Sweet Home', 'Annie Laurie', 'Barbara Allen', and 'Silver Threads Among the Gold' – they had only to ask for what they fancied. Alf played well and had a marvellous ear. If the baker or any other caller hummed the tune of a new popular song in his hearing, Alf would be playing it that night on his melodeon.

Women stood at their cottage gates, men leaned out of the inn window, and children left their play and gathered around him to listen. Often he played dance tunes, and the youths would foot it with each other as partners, for there was seldom a grown-up girl at home and the little ones they despised. So the little girls, too, had to dance with each other. One stout old woman, who was said to have been gay in her time, would come out and give them hints, or she would take a turn herself, gliding around alone, her feet hidden by her long skirts, massively graceful.

Sometimes they would sing to the dance music, and the standers-by would join in:

I have a bonnet, trimmed with blue,
Why don't you wear it? So I do.
When do you wear it? When I can,
When I go out with my young man.

My young man is gone to sea
With silver buckles on his knee,
With his blue coat and yellow hose,
And that's the way the polka goes.

Or perhaps it would be:

Step and fetch her, step and fetch her,
Step and fetch her, pretty little dear.
Do not tease her, try and please her,
Step and fetch her, pretty little dear.

And so they would dance and sing through the long summer evenings, until dusk fell and the stars came out and they all went laughing and panting home, a community simple enough to be made happy by one little boy with a melodeon.

V

AT PLAY AND AT SCHOOL

'SHALL we dance tonight or shall we have a game?' was a frequent question among the girls after Alf's arrival. Until the novelty of the dancing wore off, the old country games were eclipsed; but their day was not over. Some of the quieter girls always preferred the games, and, later, on those evenings when Alf was away, playing for dancers in other villages, they all went back to the games.

Then, beneath the long summer sunsets, the girls would gather on one of the green open spaces between the houses and bow and curtsey and sweep to and fro in their ankle-length frocks as they went through the game movements and sang the game rhymes as their mothers and grandmothers had done before them.

How long the games had been played and how they originated no one knew, for they had been handed down for a time long before living memory and accepted by each succeeding generation as a natural part of its childhood. No one inquired the meaning of the words of the game rhymes; many of the girls, indeed, barely mastered them, but went through the movements to the accompaniment of an indistinct babbling. But the rhymes had been preserved; breaking down into doggerel in places; but still sufficiently intact to have spoken to the discerning, had any such been present, of an older, sweeter country civilization than had survived, excepting in a few such fragments.

Of all the generations that had played the games, that of the 'eighties was to be the last. Already those children had one foot in the national school and one on the village green. Their children and grandchildren would have left the village green behind them; new and as yet undreamed-of pleasures and excitements would be theirs. In ten years' time the games would be neglected, and in twenty forgotten. But all through the 'eighties the games went on and seemed to the children themselves and to onlookers part of a life that always had been and always would be.

The Lark Rise children had a large repertoire, including the well-known games still met with at children's parties, such as 'Oranges and Lemons', 'London Bridge', and

'Here We Go Round the Mulberry Bush'; but also including others which appear to have been peculiar to that part of the country. Some of these were played by forming a ring, others by taking sides, and all had distinctive rhymes, which were chanted rather than sung.

The boys of the hamlet did not join in them, for the amusement was too formal and restrained for their taste, and even some of the rougher girls when playing would spoil a game, for the movements were stately and all was done by rule. Only at the end of some of the games, where the verse had deteriorated into doggerel, did the play break down into a romp. Most of the girls when playing revealed graces unsuspected in them at other times; their movements became dignified and their voices softer and sweeter than ordinarily, and when hauteur was demanded by the part, they became, as they would have said, 'regular duchesses'. It is probable that carriage and voice inflexion had been handed down with the words.

One old favourite was 'Here Come Three Tinkers'. For this all but two of the players, a big girl and a little one, joined hands in a row, and the bigger girl out took up her stand about a dozen paces in front of the row with the smaller one lying on the turf behind her feigning sleep. Then three of the line of players detached themselves and, hand in hand, tripped forward, singing:

> *Here come three tinkers, three by three,*
> *To court your daughter, fair ladye,*
> *Oh, can we have a lodging here, here, here?*
> *Oh, can we have a lodging here?*

Upon which the fair lady (pronounced 'far-la-dee') admonished her sleeping daughter:

> *Sleep, sleep, my daughter. Do not wake.*
> *Here come three tinkers you can't take.*

Then, severely, to the tinkers:

> *You cannot have a lodging here, here, here.*
> *You cannot have a lodging here.*

And the tinkers returned to the line, and three others came forward, calling themselves tailors, soldiers, sailors, gardeners, bricklayers, or policemen, according to fancy, the rhymes being sung for each three, until it was time for the climax, and, putting fresh spirit into their tones, the conquering candidates came forward, singing:

> *Here come three princes, three by three,*
> *To court your daughter fair ladye,*
> *Oh, can we have a lodging here, here, here?*
> *Oh, can we have a lodging here?*

At the mere mention of the rank of the princes the scene changed. The fair lady became all becks and nods and smiles, and, lifting up her supposedly sleeping daughter, sang:

> *Oh, wake, my daughter, wake, wake, wake.*
> *Here come three princes you can take.*

And, turning to the princes:

> *Oh, you can have a lodging here, here, here.*
> *Oh, you can have a lodging here.*

Then, finally, leading forward and presenting her daughter, she said:

> *Here is my daughter, safe and sound,*
> *And in her pocket five thousand pound,*
> *And on her finger a gay gold ring,*
> *And I'm sure she's fit to walk with a king.*

A pretty, graceful game to watch was 'Thread the Tailor's Needle'. For this two girls joined both hands and elevated them to form an arch or bridge, and the other players, in single file and holding on to each other's skirts, passed under, singing:

> *Thread the tailor's needle,*
> *Thread the tailor's needle.*
> *The tailor's blind and he can't see,*
> *So thread the tailor's needle.*

As the end of the file passed under the arch the last two girls detached themselves, took up their stand by the original two and joined their hands and elevated them, thus widening the arch, and this was repeated until the arch became a tunnel. As the file passing under grew shorter, the tune was quickened, until, towards the end, the game became a merry whirl.

A grim little game often played by the younger children was called 'Daddy'. For this a ring was formed, one of the players remaining outside it, and the outside player stalked stealthily round the silent and motionless ring and chose another girl by striking her on the shoulder. The chosen one burst from the ring and rushed round it, closely pursued by the first player, the others chanting meanwhile:

> *Round a ring to catch a king,*
> *Round a ring to catch a king,*
> *Round a ring to catch a king–*

and, as the pursuer caught up with the pursued and struck her neck with the edge of her hand:

> *Down falls Daddy!*

At the stroke on the neck the second player fell flat on the turf, beheaded, and the game continued until all were stretched on the turf.

Round *what* ring, to catch *what* king? And who was Daddy? Was the game founded on some tale dished up for the commonality of the end of one who 'nothing common did or mean'? The player did not know or care, and we can only guess. . . .

A homely game was 'The Old Woman from Cumberland'. For this a row of girls stood hand in hand with a bigger one in the middle to represent the old woman from Cumberland. Another bigger girl stood alone a few paces in front. She was known as the 'mistress'. Then the row of girls tripped forward, singing:

> *Here comes an old woman from Cumberland*
> *With all her children in her hand.*
> *And please do you want a servant to-day?*

'What can they do?' demanded the mistress as they drew up before her. Then the old woman of Cumberland detached herself and walked down the row, placing a hand on the heads of one after another of her children as she said:

> *This can brew, and this can bake,*
> *This can make a wedding cake,*
> *This can wear a gay gold ring,*
> *This can sit in the barn and sing,*
> *This can go to bed with a king,*
> *And this one can do everything.*

'Oh! I will have that one,' said the mistress, pointing to the one who could do everything, who then went over to her. The proceedings were repeated until half the girls had gone over, when the two sides had a tug-of-war.

'The Old Woman from Cumberland' was a brisk, business-like game; but most of

the rhymes of the others were long-drawn-out and sad, and saddest of all was 'Poor Mary is A-weeping', which went:

Poor Mary is a-weeping, a-weeping, a-weeping
Poor Mary is a-weeping on a bright summer's day.

And what's poor Mary a-weeping for, a-weeping for, a-weeping for?
Oh, what's poor Mary a-weeping for on a bright summer's day?

She's weeping for her own true love on a bright summer's own true love.
She's weeping for her own true love on a bright summer's day.

Then let her choose another love, another love, another love.
Then let her choose another love on a bright summer's day.

'Waly, Waly, Wallflower' ran 'Poor Mary' close in gentle melancholy; but the original verse in this seems to have broken down after the fourth line. The Lark Rise version ran:

Waly, waly, wallflower, growing up so high.
We're all maidens, we must all die,
Excepting So-and-So [naming one of the players]
And she's the youngest maid.

Then, the tune changing to a livelier air:

She can hop and she can skip,
She can play the candlestick,
Fie! Fie! Fie!
Turn your face to the wall again.

All clasping hands and jumping up and down:

All the boys in this town
*   Lead a happy life,*
Excepting So-and-So [naming some hamlet boy, not necessarily present]
*   And he wants a wife.*
A wife he shall have and a-courting he shall go,
Along with So-and-So; because he loves her so.
He kissed her, he cuddled her, he sat her on his knee,
And he said 'My dearest So-and-So, how happy we shall be.'
First he bought the frying-pan and then he bought the cradle
And then he bought the knives and forks and set them on the table.

So-and-So made a pudding, she made it very sweet,
She daren't stick the knife in till So-and-So came home at night.
Taste, So-and-So, taste, and do not be afraid,
Next Monday morning the wedding day shall be,
And the cat shall sing and the bells shall ring
And we'll all clap hands together.

Evidently in the course of the centuries 'Waly, Waly, Wallflower' had become mixed with something else. The youngest maid of the first verse would never have played the candlestick or been courted by such a lover. Her destiny was very different. But

what? . . .

As well as the country games, a few others, probably as old, but better known, were played by the hamlet children. Marbles, peg-tops, and skipping-ropes appeared in their season, and when there happened to be a ball available a game called 'Tip-it' was played. There was not always a ball to be had; for the smallest rubber one cost a penny, and pennies were scarce. Even marbles, at twenty a penny, were seldom bought, although there were a good many in circulation, for the hamlet boys were champion marble players and thought nothing of walking five or six miles on a Saturday to play with the boys of other villages and replenish their own store with their winnings. Some of them owned as trophies the scarce and valued glass marbles, called 'alleys'. These were of clear glass enclosing bright, wavy, multi-coloured threads, and they looked very handsome among the dingy-coloured clay ones. The girls skipped with any odd length of rope, usually a piece of their mothers' old clothes-lines.

A simple form of hopscotch was played, for which three lines, or steps, enclosed in an oblong were scratched in the dust. The elaborate hopscotch diagrams, resembling an astrological horoscope, still to be seen chalked on the roads in the West Country were unknown there.

'Dibs' was a girls' game, played with five small, smooth pebbles, which had to be kept in the air at the same time and caught on the back of the hand. Laura, who was clumsy with her hands, never mastered this game; nor could she play marbles or spin tops or catch balls, or play hopscotch. She was by common consent 'a duffer'. Skipping and running were her only accomplishments. . . .

After they reached school-going age, the boys no longer played with the girls, but found themselves a separate pitch on which to play marbles or spin tops or kick an old tin about by way of a football. Or they would hunt in couples along the hedgerows, shooting at birds with their catapults, climbing trees, or looking for birds' nests, mushrooms, or chestnuts, according to the season.

The birds'-nesting was a cruel sport, for not only was every egg taken from every nest they found, but the nests themselves were demolished and all the soft moss and lining feathers were left torn and scattered around on the grass and bushes.

'Oh, dear! What must the poor bird have felt when she saw that!' was Laura's cry when she came upon that, to her, saddest of all sad sights, and once she even dared to remonstrate with some boys she had found in the act. They only laughed and pushed her aside. To them, the idea that anything so small as a mother

95

chaffinch could feel was ridiculous. They were thinking of the lovely long string of threaded eggshells, blue and speckled and pearly white, they hoped to collect and hang up at home as an ornament. The tiny whites and yolks which would come from the eggs when blown they would make their mothers whip up and stir into their own cup of tea as a delicacy, and their mothers would be pleased and say what kind, thoughtful boys they had, for they, like the boys, did not consider the birds' point of view.

No one in authority told them that such wholesale robbery of birds' nests was cruel. Even the Rector, when he called at the cottages, would admire the collections and sometimes even condescend to accept a rare specimen. Ordinary country people at that time, though not actively cruel to animals, were indifferent to their sufferings. 'Where there's no sense there's no feeling,' they would say when they had hurt some creature by accident or through carelessness. By sense they meant wits or understanding, and these they imagined purely human attributes.

A few birds were sacred. No boy would rob a robin's or a wren's nest; nor would they have wrecked a swallow's nest if they could have reached one, for they believed that:

> The robin and the wrens
> Be God Almighty's friends.
> And the martin and the swallow
> Be God Almighty's birds to follow.

And those four were safe from molestation. Their cruelty to the other birds and to some other animals was due to an utter lack of imagination, not to bad-heartedness. When, a little later, country boys were taught in school to show mercy to animals and especially to birds, one egg only from a clutch became the general rule. Then came the splendid Boy Scout movement, which has done more than all the Preservation of Wild Birds Acts to prevent the wholesale raiding of nests, by teaching the boys mercy and kindness. . . .

In one way and another a bird, or a few birds, were a regular feature of the hamlet menu. But there were birds and birds. 'Do you think you could fancy a bird, me dear?' a man would say to his ailing wife or child, and if they thought they would the bird would appear; but it would not be a sparrow, or even a thrush or a lark. It would be a much bigger bird with a plump breast; but it would never be named and no feathers would be left lying about by which to identify it. The hamlet men were not habitual poachers. They called poaching 'a mug's game' and laughed at those who practised it. 'One month in quod and one out,' as they said. But, when the necessity arose, they knew where the game birds were and how to get them.

Edmund and Laura once witnessed a neat bit of poaching. They had climbed a ladder they had found set against the side of a haystack which had been unthatched, ready for removal, and, after an exciting hour of sticking out their heads and making faces to represent gargoyles on a tower, they were lying, hidden from below, while the men on their way home from work passed along the footpath beneath the rick.

It was near sunset and the low, level light searched the path and the stubble and aftermath on either side of it. The men sauntered along in twos and threes, smoking and talking, then disappeared, group by group, over the stile at the farther side of the field. Just as the last group was nearing the stile and the children were breathing a sigh of relief at not having been seen and scolded, a hare broke from one of the hedges and went bounding and capering across the field in the headlong way hares have. It looked for a moment as if it would land under the feet of the last group of men, who were nearing the stile; but, suddenly, it scented danger and drew up and squatted motionless behind a tuft of green clover a few feet from the pathway. Just then one of the men fell behind to tie his bootlace: the others passed over the stile. The moment they were out of sight, in one movement, the man left behind rose and flung himself sideways over the clover clump where the hare was hiding. There was a short scuffle, a slight raising of dust; then the limp form was pressed into a dinner-basket, and, after a good look round to make sure his action had not been observed, the man followed his workmates.

School began at nine o'clock, but the hamlet children set out on their mile-and-a-half walk there as soon as possible after their seven o'clock breakfast, partly because they liked plenty of time to play on the road and partly because their mothers wanted them out of the way before house-cleaning began.

Up the long, straight road they straggled, in twos and threes and in gangs, their flat, rush dinner-baskets over their shoulders and their shabby little coats on their arms against rain. In cold weather some of them carried two hot potatoes which had been in the oven, or in the ashes, all night, to warm their hands on the way and to serve as a light lunch on arrival.

They were strong, lusty children, let loose from

control, and there was plenty of shouting, quarrelling, and often fighting among them. In more peaceful moments they would squat in the dust of the road and play marbles, or sit on a stone heap and play dibs with pebbles, or climb into the hedges after birds' nests or blackberries, or to pull long trails of bryony to wreathe round their hats. In winter they would slide on the ice on the puddles, or make snowballs – soft ones for their friends, and hard ones with a stone inside for their enemies.

After the first mile or so the dinner-baskets would be raided; or they would creep through the bars of the padlocked field gates for turnips to pare with the teeth and munch, or for handfuls of green pea shucks, or ears of wheat, to rub out the sweet, milky grain between the hands and devour. In spring they ate the young green from the hawthorn hedges, which they called 'bread and cheese', and sorrel leaves from the wayside, which they called 'sour grass', and in autumn there was an abundance of haws

and blackberries and sloes and crab-apples for them to feast upon. There was always something to eat, and they ate, not so much because they were hungry as from habit and relish of the wild food. . . .

It has been said that every child is born a little savage and has to be civilized. The process of civilization had not gone very far with some of the hamlet children; although one civilization had them in hand at home and another at school, they were able to throw off both on the road between the two places and revert to a state of Nature. A favourite amusement with these was to fall in a body upon some unoffending companion, usually a small girl in a clean frock, and to 'run her', as they called it. This meant chasing her until they caught her, then dragging her down and sitting upon her, tearing her clothes, smudging her face, and tousling her hair in the process. She might scream and cry and say she would 'tell on' them; they took no notice until, tiring of the sport, they would run whooping off, leaving her sobbing and exhausted.

The persecuted one never 'told on' them, even when reproved by the schoolmistress for her dishevelled condition, for she knew that, if she had, there would have been a worse 'running' to endure on the way home, and one that went to the tune of:

> Tell-tale tit!
> Cut her tongue a-slit,
> And every little puppy-dog
> Shall have a little bit!

It was no good telling the mothers either, for it was the rule of the hamlet never to interfere in the children's quarrels. 'Let 'em fight it out among theirselves,' the woman would say; and if a child complained the only response would be: 'You must've been doin' summat to them. If you'd've left them alone, they'd've left you alone; so don't come bringing your tales home to me!' It was harsh schooling; but the majority seemed to thrive upon it, and the few quieter and more sensitive children soon learned either to start early and get to school first, or to linger behind, dipping under bushes and lurking inside field gates until the main body had passed. . . .

Although they started to school so early, the hamlet children took so much time on the way that the last quarter of a mile was always a race, and they would rush, panting and dishevelled, into school just as the bell stopped, and the other children, spick and span, fresh from their mothers' hands, would eye them sourly. 'That gipsy lot from Lark Rise!' they would murmur.

Fordlow National School was a small grey one-storied building, standing at the cross-roads at the entrance to the village. The one large classroom which served all purposes was well lighted with several windows, including the large one which filled the end of the building which faced the road. Beside, and joined on to the school, was a tiny two-roomed cottage for the schoolmistress, and beyond that a playground with birch trees and turf, bald in places, the whole being enclosed within pointed, white-painted palings.

The only other building in sight was a row of model cottages occupied by the shepherd, the blacksmith, and other superior farm-workers. The school had probably been built at the same time as the houses and by the same model landlord; for, though it would seem a hovel compared to a modern council school, it must at that time have been fairly up-to-date. It had a lobby with pegs for clothes, boys' and girls' earth-closets, and a backyard with fixed wash-basins, although there was no water laid on. The water supply was contained in a small bucket, filled every morning by the old woman who cleaned the schoolroom, and every morning she grumbled because the children had been so extravagant that she had to 'fill 'un again'.

The average attendance was about forty-five. Ten or twelve of the children lived near the school, a few others came from cottages in the fields, and the rest were the Lark Rise children. Even then, to an outsider, it would have appeared a quaint, old-fashioned little gathering; the girls in their ankle-length frocks and long, straight pinafores, with their hair strained back from their brows and secured on their crowns by a ribbon or black tape or a bootlace; the bigger boys in corduroys and hobnailed boots, and the smaller ones in home-made sailor suits or, until they were six or seven, in petticoats.

Baptismal names were such as the children's parents and grandparents had borne. The fashion in Christian names was changing; babies were being christened Mabel and Gladys and Doreen and Percy and Stanley; but the change was too recent to have affected the names of the older children. Mary Ann, Sarah Ann, Eliza, Martha, Annie, Jane, Amy, and Rose were favourite girls' names. There was a Mary Ann in almost every family, and Eliza was nearly as popular. But none of them were called by their proper names. Mary Ann and Sarah Ann were contracted to Mar'ann and Sar'ann. Mary, apart from Ann, had, by stages, descended through Molly and Polly to Poll. Eliza had become Liza, then Tiza, then Tize; Martha was Mat or Pat; Jane was Jin; and every Amy had at least one 'Aim' in life, of which she had constant reminder. The few more uncommon names were also distorted. Two sisters named at the font Beatrice and Agnes, went through life as Beat and Agg, Laura was Lor, or Low, and Edmund was Ned or Ted.

Laura's mother disliked this cheapening of names and named her third child May, thinking it would not lend itself to a diminutive. However, while still in her cradle, the child became Mayie among the neighbours. . . .

The schoolmistress in charge of the Fordlow school at the beginning of the 'eighties

had held that position for fifteen years and seemed to her pupils as much a fixture as the school building; but for most of that time she had been engaged to the squire's head gardener and her long reign was drawing to a close.

She was, at that time, about forty, and was a small, neat little body with a pale, slightly pock-marked face, snaky black curls hanging down to her shoulders, and eyebrows arched into a perpetual inquiry. She wore in school stiffly starched, holland aprons with bibs, one embroidered with red one week, and one with blue the next, and was seldom seen without a posy of flowers pinned on her breast and another tucked into her hair. . . .

Reading, writing, and arithmetic were the principal subjects, with a Scripture lesson every morning, and needlework every afternoon for the girls. There was no assistant mistress; Governess taught all the classes simultaneously, assisted only by two monitors – ex-scholars, aged about twelve, who were paid a shilling a week each for their services.

Every morning at ten o'clock the Rector arrived to take the older children for Scripture. He was a parson of the old school; a commanding figure, tall and stout, with white hair, ruddy cheeks and an aristocratically beaked nose, and he was as far as possible removed by birth, education, and worldly circumstances from the lambs of his flock. He spoke to them from a great height, physical, mental, and spiritual. 'To order myself lowly and reverently before my betters' was the clause he underlined in the Church Catechism, for had he not been divinely appointed pastor and master to those little rustics and was it not one of his chief duties to teach them to realize this? As a man, he was kindly disposed – a giver of blankets and coals at Christmas, and of soup and milk puddings to the sick.

His lesson consisted of Bible reading, turn and turn about round the class, of reciting from memory the names of the kings of Israel and repeating the Church Catechism. After that, he would deliver a little lecture on morals and behaviour. The children must not lie or steal or be discontented or envious. God had placed them just where they were in the social order and given them their own special work to do; to envy others or to try to change their own lot in life was a sin of which he hoped they would never be guilty. From his lips the children heard nothing of that God who is Truth and Beauty and Love; but they learned for him and repeated to him long passages from the Authorized Version, thus laying up treasure for themselves; so the lessons, in spite of much aridity, were valuable.

Scripture over and the Rector bowed and curtsied out of the door, ordinary lessons began. Arithmetic was considered the most important of the subjects taught, and those who were good at figures ranked high in their classes. It was very simple arithmetic, extending only to the first four rules, with the money sums, known as 'bills of parcels', for the most advanced pupils.

The writing lesson consisted of the copying of copperplate maxims: 'A fool and his money are soon parted'; 'Waste not, want not'; 'Count ten before you speak', and so on. Once a week composition would be set, usually in the form of writing a letter describing some recent event. This was regarded chiefly as a spelling test.

History was not taught formally; but history readers were in use containing such picturesque stories as those of King Alfred and the cakes, King Canute commanding the waves, the loss of the White Ship, and Raleigh spreading his cloak for Queen Elizabeth.

There were no geography readers and, excepting what could be gleaned from the descriptions of different parts of the world in the ordinary readers, no geography was taught. But, for some reason or other, on the walls of the schoolroom were hung splendid maps: The World, Europe, North America, South America, England, Ireland, and Scotland. During long waits in class for her turn to read, or to have her copy or sewing examined, Laura would gaze on these maps until the shapes of the countries with their islands and inlets became photographed on her brain. Baffin Bay and the land around the poles were especially fascinating to her.

Once a day, at whatever hour the poor, overworked mistress could find time, a class would be called out to toe the chalked semicircle on the floor for a reading lesson. This lesson, which should have been pleasant, for the reading matter was good, was tedious in the extreme. Many of the children read so slowly and haltingly that Laura, who was impatient by nature, longed to take hold of their words and drag them out of their mouths, and it often seemed to her that her own turn to read would never come. As often as she could do so without being detected, she would turn over and peep between the pages of her own *Royal Reader*, and, studiously holding the book to her nose, pretend to be following the lesson while she was pages ahead.

There was plenty there to enthral any child: 'The Skater Chased by Wolves'; The Siege of Torquilstone', from *Ivanhoe*; Fenimore Cooper's *Prairie on Fire*; and Washington Irving's *Capture of Wild Horses*.

Then there were fascinating descriptions of such far-apart places as Greenland and the Amazon; of the Pacific Ocean with its fairy islands and coral reefs; the snows of Hudson Bay Territory and the sterile heights of the Andes. Best of all she loved the description of the Himalayas, which began: 'Northward of the great plain of India, and along its whole extent, towers the sublime mountain region of the Himalayas, ascending gradually until it terminates in a long range of summits wrapped in perpetual snow.'. . .

Those children who read fluently, and there were several of them in every class, read in a monotonous sing-song, without expression, and apparently without interest. Yet there were very few really stupid children in the school, as is proved by the success of many of them in after life, and though few were interested in their lessons, they nearly all showed an intelligent interest in other things – the boys in field work and crops and cattle and agricultural machinery; the girls in dress, other people's love affairs and domestic details.

It is easy to imagine the education authorities of that day, when drawing up the scheme for that simple but sound education, saying, 'Once teach them to read and they will hold the key to all knowledge.' But the scheme did not work out. If the children, by the time they left school, could read well enough to read the newspaper and perhaps an occasional book for amusement, and write well enough to write their own letters, they had no wish to go farther. Their interest was not in books, but in life, and especially the life that lay immediately about them. At school they worked unwillingly, upon compulsion, and the life of the schoolmistress was a hard one.

As Miss Holmes went from class to class, she carried the cane and laid it upon the desk before her; not necessarily for use, but as a reminder, for some of the bigger boys were very unruly. She punished by a smart stroke on each hand. 'Put out your hand,' she would say, and some boys would openly spit on each hand before proffering it. Others murmured and muttered before and after a caning and threatened to 'tell me feyther'; but she remained calm and cool, and after the punishment had been inflicted

there was a marked improvement – for a time.

It must be remembered that in those days a boy of eleven was nearing the end of his school life. Soon he would be at work; already he felt himself nearly a man and too old for petticoat government. Moreover, those were country boys, wild and rough, and many of them as tall as she was. Those who had failed to pass Standard IV and so could not leave school until they were eleven, looked upon that last year as a punishment inflicted upon them by the school authorities and behaved accordingly. In this they were encouraged by their parents, for a certain section of these resented their boys being kept at school when they might be earning. 'What do our young Alf want wi' a lot o' book-larnin'?' they would say. 'He can read and write and add up as much money as he's ever likely to get. What more do he want?' Then a neighbour of more advanced views would tell them: 'A good education's everything in these days. You can't get on in the world if you ain't had one,' for they read their newspapers and new ideas were percolating, though slowly. It was only the second generation to be forcibly fed with the fruit of the tree of knowledge: what wonder if it did not always agree with it.

Meanwhile, Miss Holmes carried her cane about with her. A poor method of enforcing discipline, according to modern educational ideas: but it served. It may be that she and her like all over the country at that time were breaking up the ground that other, later comers to the field, with a knowledge of child psychology and with tradition and experiment behind them, might sow the good seed.

She seldom used the cane on the girls and still more seldom on the infants. Standing in a corner with their hands on their heads was their punishment. She gave little treats and encouragements, too, and, although the children called her 'Susie' behind her back, they really liked and respected her. Many times there came a knock at the door and a smartly dressed girl on holidays, or a tall young soldier on leave, in his scarlet tunic and pill-box cap, looked in 'to see Governess'.

That Laura could already read when she went to school was never discovered. 'Do you know your ABC?' the mistress asked her on the first morning. 'Come, let me hear you say it: A – B – C –'

'A – B – C –' Laura began; but when she got to F she stumbled, for she had never memorized the letters in order. So she was placed in the class known as 'the babies' and joined in chanting the alphabet from A to Z.

Once started, they were like a watch wound up, and went on alone for hours. The mistress, with all the other classes on her hands, had no time to teach the babies, although she always had a smile for them when she passed and any disturbance or cessation of the chanting would bring her down to them at once. Even the monitors were usually engaged in giving out dictation to the older children, or in hearing tables or spelling repeated; but, in the afternoon, one of the bigger girls, usually the one who was the poorest needlewoman (it was always Laura in later years) would come down from her own form to point to and name each letter on a wall-sheet, the little ones repeating them after her. Then she would teach them to form pot-hooks and hangers, and, afterwards, letters, on their slates, and this went on for years, as it seemed to Laura, but perhaps it was only one year.

At the end of that time the class was examined and those who knew and could form their letters were moved up into the official 'Infants'. Laura, who by this time was reading *Old St Paul's* at home, simply romped through this Little-Go; but without credit, for it was said she 'gabbled' her letters, and her writing was certainly poor.

It was not until she reached Standard I that her troubles really began. Arithmetic was the subject by which the pupils were placed, and as Laura could not grasp the simplest rule with such small help as the mistress had time to give, she did not even know how to begin working out the sums and was permanently at the bottom of the class. At needlework in the afternoon she was no better. The girls around her in class were making pinafores for themselves, putting in tiny stitches and biting off their cotton like grown women, while she was still struggling with her first hemming strip. And a dingy, crumpled strip it was before she had done with it, punctuated throughout its length with blood spots where she had pricked her fingers.

'Oh, Laura! What a dunce you are!' Miss Holmes used to say every time she examined it, and Laura really was the dunce of the school in those two subjects. However, as time went on, she improved a little, and managed to pass her standard every year with moderate success until she came to Standard V and could go no farther, for that was the highest in the school. By that time the other children she had worked with had left, excepting one girl named Emily Rose, who was an only child and lived in a lonely cottage far out in the fields. For two years Standard V consisted of Laura and Emily Rose. They did few lessons and those few mostly those they could learn from books by themselves, and much of their time was spent in teaching the babies and assisting the schoolmistress generally.

That mistress was not Miss Holmes. She had married her head gardener while Laura was still in the Infants and gone to live in a pretty old cottage which she had renamed 'Malvern Villa'. Immediately after her had come a young teacher, fresh from her training college, with all the latest educational ideas. She was a bright, breezy girl, keen on reform and anxious to be a friend as well as a teacher to her charges.

She came too early. The human material she had to work on was not ready for such methods. On the first morning she began a little speech, meaning to take the children into her confidence:

'Good morning, children. My name is Matilda Annie Higgs, and I want us all to be friends –' A giggling murmur ran round the school. 'Matilda Annie! Matilda Annie! Did she say Higgs or pigs?' The name made direct appeal to their crude sense of humour, and, as to the offer of friendship, they scented weakness in that, coming from one whose office it was to rule. Thenceforth, Miss Higgs might drive her pigs in the rhyme they shouted in her hearing; but she could neither drive nor lead her pupils. They hid her cane, filled her inkpot with water, put young frogs in her desk, and asked her silly, unnecessary questions about their work. When she answered them, they all coughed in chorus.

The girls were as bad as the boys. Twenty times in one afternoon a hand would shoot upward and it would be: 'Please, miss, can I have this or that from the needlework box?' and poor Miss Higgs, trying to teach a class at the other end of the room, would come and unlock and search the box for something they had already and had hidden.

Several times she appealed to them to show more consideration. Once she burst into tears before the whole school. She told the woman who cleaned that she had never dreamed there were such children anywhere. They were little savages.

One afternoon, when a pitched battle was raging among the big boys in class and the mistress was calling imploringly for order, the Rector appeared in the doorway.

'Silence!' he roared.

The silence was immediate and profound, for they knew he was not one to be trifled with. Like Gulliver among the Lilliputians, he strode into the midst of them, his face flushed with anger, his eyes flashing blue fire. 'Now, what is the meaning of this disgraceful uproar?'

Some of the younger children began to cry; but one look in their direction froze them into silence and they sat, wide-eyed and horrified, while he had the whole class out and caned each boy soundly, including those who had taken no part in the fray. Then, after a heated discourse in which he reminded the children of their lowly position in life and the twin duties of gratitude to and respect towards their superiors, school was dismissed. Trembling hands seized coats and dinner-baskets and frightened little figures made a dash for the gate. But the big boys who had caused the trouble showed a different spirit. 'Who cares for him?' they muttered, 'Who cares? Who cares? He's only an old parson!' Then, when safely out of the playground, one voice shouted:

Old Charley-wag! Old Charley-wag!
Ate the pudden and gnawed the bag!

The other children expected the heavens to fall; for Mr Ellison's Christian name was Charles. The shout was meant for him and was one of defiance. He did not recognize it as such. There were several Charleses in the school, and it must have been inconceivable to him that his own Christian name should be intended. Nothing happened, and, after a few moments of tense silence, the rebels trooped off to get their own account of the affair in first at home.

After that, it was not long before the station fly stood at the school gate and Miss Higgs's trunk and bundles and easy-chair were hauled on top. Back came the married Miss Holmes, now Mrs Tenby. Girls curtsied again and boys pulled their forelocks. It was 'Yes, ma'am', and 'No, ma'am', and 'What did you please to say, ma'am?' once more. But either she did not wish to teach again permanently or the education authorities already had a rule against employing married-women teachers, for she only remained a few weeks until a new mistress was engaged.

This turned out to be a sweet, frail-looking, grey-haired, elderly lady named Miss Shepherd, and a gentle shepherd she proved to her flock. Unfortunately, she was but a poor disciplinarian, and the struggle to maintain some degree of order wore her almost to shreds. Again there was always a buzz of whispering in class; stupid and unnecessary questions were asked, and too long intervals elapsed between the word of command and the response. But, unlike Miss Higgs, she did not give up. Perhaps she could not afford to do so at her age and with an invalid sister living with and dependent upon her. She ruled, if she can be said to have ruled at all, by love and patience and ready forgiveness. In time, even the blackest of her sheep realized this and kept within certain limits; just sufficient order was maintained to avoid scandal, and the school settled down under her mild rule for five or six years. . . .

She taught the children that it was not what a man or woman had, but what they

III

were which mattered. That poor people's souls are as valuable and that their hearts may be as good and their minds as capable of cultivation as those of the rich. She even hinted that on the material plane people need not necessarily remain always upon one level. Some boys, born of poor parents, had struck out for themselves and become great men, and everybody had respected them for rising upon their own merits. She would read them the lives of some of these so-called self-made men (there were no women, Laura noticed!) and though their circumstances were too far removed from those of her hearers for them to inspire the ambition she hoped to awaken, they must have done something to widen their outlook on life.

Meanwhile the ordinary lessons went on. Reading, writing, arithmetic, all a little less rather than more well taught and mastered than formerly. In needlework there was a definite falling off. Miss Shepherd was not a great needle-woman herself and was inclined to cut down the sewing time to make way for other work. Infinitesimal stiches no longer provoked delighted exclamations, but more often a 'Child! You will ruin your eyes!' As the bigger girls left who in their time had won county prizes, the standard of the output declined, until, from being known as one of the first needlework schools in the district, Fordlow became one of the last.

Her Majesty's Inspector of Schools came once a year on a date of which previous notice had been given. There was no singing or quarrelling on the way to school that morning. The children, in clean pinafores and well blackened boots, walked deep in thought; or, with open spelling or table books in hand, tried to make up in an hour for all their wasted yesterdays.

Although the date of 'Inspector's' visit had been notified, the time had not. Some years he would come to Fordlow in the morning; other years in the afternoon, having examined another school earlier. So, after prayers, copybooks were given out and the children settled down for a long wait. A few of the more stolid, leaning forward with tongues slightly protruding, would copy laboriously, 'Lightly on the up-strokes, heavy on the down', but most of the children were too apprehensive even to attempt to work and the mistress did not urge them, for she felt even more apprehensive herself and did not want nervously executed copies to witness against her.

Ten – eleven – the hands of the clock dragged on, and forty-odd hearts might almost be heard thumping when at last came the sound of wheels crunching on gravel and two top hats and the top of a whip appeared outside the upper panes of the large end window.

Her Majesty's Inspector was an elderly clergyman, a little man with an immense paunch and tiny grey eyes like gimlets. He had the reputation of being 'strict', but that was a mild way of describing his autocratic demeanour and scathing judgement. His voice was an exasperated roar and his criticism was a blend of outraged learning and sarcasm. Fortunately, nine out of ten of his examinees were proof against the latter. He looked at the rows of children as if he hated them and at the mistress as if he despised her. The Assistant Inspector was also a clergyman, but younger, and, in comparison, almost human. Black eyes and very red lips shone through the bushiness of the whiskers which almost covered his face. The children in the lower classes, which he examined, were considered fortunate.

The mistress did not have to teach a class in front of the great man, as later; her part was to put out the books required and to see that the pupils had the pens and paper they needed. Most of the time she hovered about the Inspector, replying in low tones to his scathing remarks, or, with twitching lips, smiling encouragement at any child who happened to catch her eye.

What kind of a man the Inspector really was it is impossible to say. He may have been a great scholar, a good parish priest, and a good friend and neighbour to people of his own class. One thing, however, is certain, he did not care for or understand children, at least not national school children. In homely language, he was the wrong man for the job. The very sound of his voice scattered the few wits of the less gifted, and even those who could have done better were too terrified in his presence to be able to collect their thoughts to keep their hands from trembling.

But, slowly as the hands of the clock seemed to move, the afternoon wore on. Classes came out and toed the chalk line to read; other classes bent over their sums, or wrote letters to grandmothers describing imaginary summer holidays. Some wrote to the great man's dictation pieces full of hard spelling words. One year he made the confusion of their minds doubly confused by adopting the, to them, new method of giving out the stops by name: 'Water-fowl and other aquatic birds dwell on their banks semicolon while on the surface of the placid water float the wide-spreading leaves of the *Victoria regia* comma and other lilies and water dash plants full stop.'

Of course, they all wrote the names of the stops, which, together with their spelling,

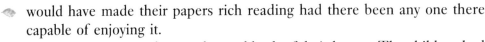

would have made their papers rich reading had there been any one there capable of enjoying it.

The composition class made a sad hash of their letters. The children had been told beforehand that they must fill at least one page, so they wrote in a very large hand and spaced their lines well; but what to say was the difficulty! One year the Inspector, observing a small boy sitting bolt upright gazing before him, called savagely: 'Why are you not writing – you at the end of the row? You have your pen and your paper, have you not?'

'Yes, thank you, sir.'

'Then why are you idling?'

'Please, sir, I was only thinking what to say.'

A grunt was the only answer. What other was possible from one who must have known well that pen, ink, and paper were no good without at least a little thinking.

Once he gave out to Laura's class two verses of *The Ancient Mariner,* reading them through first, then dictating them very slowly, with an air of aloof disdain, and yet rolling the lines on his tongue as if he relished them:

'All in a hot and copper sky,' he bawled. Then his voice softened. So perhaps there was another side to his nature.

At last the ordeal was over. No one would know who had passed and who had not for a fortnight; but that did not trouble the children at all. They crept like mice from the presence, and then, what shouting and skipping and tumbling each other in the dust as soon as they were out of sight and hearing!

When the papers arrived and the examination results were read out it was surprising to find what a number had passed. The standard must have been very low, for the children had never been taught some of the work set, and in what they had learned nervous dread had prevented them for reaching their usual poor level. . . .

There was a good deal of jealousy and unkindness among the parents over the passes and still more over the one annual prize for Scripture. Those whose children had not done well in examinations would never believe that the success of others was due to merit. The successful ones were spoken of as 'favourites' and disliked. 'You ain't a-goin' to tell me that that young So-and-So did any better n'r our Jim,' some disappointed mother would say. 'Stands to reason that what he could do our Jimmy could do, *and* better, too. Examinations are all a lot of humbug, if you asks me.' The parents of those who had passed were almost apologetic. ''Tis all luck,' they would say. 'Our Tize happened to hit it this time; next year it'll be your Alice's turn.' They showed no pleasure in any small success their own children might have. Indeed, it is doubtful if they felt any, except in the case of a boy who, having passed the fourth standard, could leave school and start work. Their ideal for themselves and their children was to keep to the level of the normal. To them outstanding ability was no better than

outstanding stupidity. . . .

At that time the position of a village schoolmistress was a trying one socially. Perhaps it is still trying in some places, for it is not many years ago that the President of a Women's Institute wrote: 'We are very democratic here. Our Committee consists of three ladies, three women, and the village schoolmistress.' That mistress, though neither lady nor woman, was still placed. In the 'eighties the schoolmistress was so nearly a new institution that a vicar's wife, in a real dilemma said: 'I should like to ask Miss So-and-So to tea; but do I ask her to kitchen or dining-room tea?'

Miss Holmes had settled that question herself when she became engaged to the squire's gardener. Miss Shepherd was more ambitious socially. Indeed, democratic as she was in theory, the dear soul was in practice a little snobbish. She courted the notice of the betters, though, she was wont to declare, they were only betters when they were

better men and women. An invitation to tea at the Rectory was, to her, something to be fished for before and talked about afterwards, and when the daughter of a poor, but aristocratic local family set up as a music teacher, Miss Shepherd at once decided to learn the violin.

Laura was once the delighted witness of a funny little display of this weakness. It was the day of the school treat at the Manor House, and the children had met at the school and were being marched, two and two, through garden and shrubbery paths to the back door. Other guests, such as the curate, the doctor's widow, and the daughters of the rich farmer, who were to have tea in the drawing-room while the children feasted in the servants' hall, were going to the front door.

Now, Miss Holmes had always marched right in with her pupils and sipped her own tea and nibbled her cake between attending to their wants; but Miss Shepherd was more ambitious. When the procession reached a point where the shrubbery path crossed the main drive which led to the front door, she paused and considered; then said, 'I think I will go to the front door, dears. I want to see how well you can behave without me,' and off she branched up the drive in her best brown frock, tight little velvet hip-length jacket, and long fur boa bound like a snake round her neck, followed by at least one pair of cynically smiling little eyes.

She had the satisfaction of ringing the front-door bell and drinking tea in the drawing-room; but it was a short-lived triumph. In a very few minutes she was out in the servants' hall, passing bread and butter to her charges and whispering to one of her monitors that 'Dear Mrs Bracewell gave me my tea first, because, as she said, she knew I was anxious to get back to my children.'

Squire himself called at the school once a year; but nobody felt nervous when his red, jovial face appeared in the doorway, and smiles broke out all around when he told

his errand. He was arranging a concert, to take place in the schoolroom, and would like some of the children to sing. He took his responsibilities less seriously than his mother did hers; spending most of his days roaming the fields and spinneys with a gun under his arm and a brace of spaniels at his heels, leaving her to manage house and gardens and what was left of the family estate, as well as to support the family dignity. His one indoor accomplishment was playing the banjo and singing Negro songs. He had trained a few of the village youths to support him in his Negro Minstrel Troupe, which always formed the backbone of the annual concert programme. A few other items were contributed by his and his mother's friends and the gaps were filled up by the schoolchildren.

So, after his visit, the school became animated. What should be sung and who should sing it were the questions of the moment. Finally, it was arranged that everybody should sing something. Even Laura, who had neither voice nor ear for

music, was to join in the communal songs.

They sang, very badly, mildly pretty spring and Nature songs from the *School Song Book*, such as they had sung the year before and the year before that, some of them actually the same songs. One year Miss Shepherd thought it 'would be nice' to sing a Primrose League song to 'please Squire'. One verse ran:

> *O come, ye Tories, all unite*
> *To bear the Primrose badge with might,*
> *And work and hope and strive and fight*
> *And pray may God defend the right.*

When Laura's father heard this, he wrote a stiffly polite little note to the mistress, saying that, as a Liberal of pronounced views, he could not allow a child of his to sing such a song. Laura did not tell him she had already been asked to sing very softly, not to put the other singers out of tune. 'Just move your lips, dear,' the mistress had said. Laura, in fact, was to have gone on to help dress the stage, where all the girls who were taking part in the programme sat in a row throughout the performance, forming a background for the soloists. That year she had the pleasure of sitting among the audience and hearing the criticism, as well as seeing the stage and listening to the programme. A good three-pennyworth ('children, half-price').

When the great night came, the whole population of the neighbourhood assembled, for it was the only public entertainment of the year. Squire and his Negro Minstrel Troupe was the great attraction. They went on, dressed in red and blue, their hands and faces blackened with burnt cork, and rattled their bones and cracked their jokes and sang such songs as:

> *A friend of Darwin's came to me*
> *A million years ago said he*
> *You had a tail and no great toe.*
> *I answered him, 'That may be so,*
> *But I've one now, I'll let you know—*
> *G-r-r-r-r-r out!'*

Very few in the audience had heard of Darwin or his theory; but they all knew what 'G-R-R-R-R-R out!' meant, especially when emphasized by a kick on Tom Binns's backside by Squire's boot. The schoolroom rocked. 'I pretty well busted me sides wi' laughin',' they said afterwards.

After the applause had died down, a little bell would ring and a robust curate from a neighbouring village would announce the next item. Most of these were piano pieces, played singly, or as duets, by young ladies in white evening frocks, cut in a modest V at the neck, and white kid gloves reaching to the

elbow. As their contributions to the programme were announced, they would rise from the front seat in the audience; a gentleman – two gentlemen – would spring forward, and between them hand the fair performer up the three shallow steps which led to the platform and hand her over to yet another gentleman, who led her to the piano and held her gloves and fan and turned her music pages.

'Tinkle, tinkle, tinkle' went the piano, and 'Warble, warble, warble' went the voices, as the performers worked their conscientious way through the show piano pieces and popular drawing-room ballads of the moment. Each performer was greeted and dismissed with a round of applause, which served the double purpose of encouraging the singer and relieving the boredom of the audience. Youths and young men in the back seats would sometimes carry this too far, drowning the programme with their stamping and shouting until they had to be reprimanded, when they would subside sulkily, complaining, 'Us've paid our sixpences, ain't we?'. . .

Going home with lanterns swinging down the long dark road, the groups would discuss the evening's entertainment. Squire's Minstrels and the curate's songs were always unreservedly praised and the young ladies' performances were tolerated, although, often, a man would complain, 'I don't know if I be goin' deaf, or what; but I couldn't hear a dommed word any of 'em said.' As to the school-children's efforts, criticism was applied more to how they looked than to their musical performance. Those who had scuffled or giggled, or even blushed, heard of it from their parents, while such remarks were frequent as: 'Got up to kill, that young Mary Ann Parish was!' or 'I declare I could see the hem o' young Rose Mitchell's breeches showin',' or 'That Em Tuffrey made a poor show. Whatever wer' her mother a thinkin' on?' Taken all in all, they enjoyed the concert almost as much as their grandchildren enjoy the cinema. . . .

VI
FESTIVALS

IF the Lark Rise people had been asked their religion, the answer of nine out of ten would have been 'Church of England', for practically all of them were christened, married, and buried as such, although, in adult life, few went to church between the baptisms of their offspring. The children were shepherded there after Sunday school and about a dozen of their elders attended regularly; the rest stayed at home, the women cooking and nursing, and the men, after an elaborate Sunday toilet, which included shaving and cutting each other's hair and much puffing and splashing with buckets of water, but stopped short before lacing up boots or putting on a collar and tie, spent the rest of the day eating, sleeping, reading the newspaper, and strolling round to see how their neighbours' pigs and gardens were looking.

There were a few keener spirits. The family at the inn was Catholic and was up and off to early Mass in the next village before others had turned over in bed for an extra Sunday morning snooze. There were also three Methodist families which met in one of their cottages on Sunday evenings for prayer and praise; but most of these attended church as well, thus earning for themselves the name of 'Devil dodgers'.

Every Sunday, morning and afternoon, the two cracked, flat-toned bells at the church in the mother village called the faithful to worship. *Ding-dong, Ding-dong, Ding-dong,* they went, and, when they heard them, the hamlet churchgoers hurried across fields and over stiles, for the Parish Clerk was always threatening to lock the church door when the bells stopped and those outside might stop outside for all he cared.

With the Fordlow cottagers, the Squire's and farmer's families and maids, the Rectory people and the hamlet contingent, the congregation averaged about thirty. Even with this small number, the church was fairly well filled, for it was a tiny place, about the size of a barn, with nave and chancel only, no side aisles. The interior was almost as bare as a barn, with its grey, roughcast walls, plain-glass windows, and flagstone floor. The cold, damp, earthy odour common to old and unheated churches pervaded the atmosphere, with occasional whiffs of a more unpleasant nature said to proceed from the stacks of mouldering bones in the vault beneath. Who had been buried there, or when, was unknown, for, excepting one ancient and mutilated brass in the wall by the font, there were but two memorial tablets, both of comparatively recent date. The church, like the village, was old and forgotten, and those buried in the vault, who must have once been people of importance, had not left even a name. Only the stained glass window over the altar, glowing jewel-like amidst the cold greyness, the broken piscina within the altar rails, and a tall broken shaft of what had been a cross in the churchyard, remained to witness mutely to what once had been.

The Squire's and clergyman's families had pews in the chancel, with backs to the wall on either side, and between them stood two long benches for the schoolchildren, well under the eyes of authority. Below the steps down into the nave stood the harmonium, played by the clergyman's daughter, and round it was ranged the choir of small schoolgirls. Then came the rank and file of the congregation, nicely graded, with the farmer's family in the front row, then the Squire's gardener and coachman, the schoolmistress, the maidservants, and the cottagers, with the Parish Clerk at the back to keep order. . . .

Mr Ellison in the pulpit was the Mr Ellison of the Scripture lessons, plus a white surplice. To him, his congregation were but children of a larger growth, and he preached as he taught. A favourite theme was the duty of regular churchgoing. He would hammer away at that for forty-five minutes, never seeming to realize that he was preaching to the absent, that all those present were regular attendants, and that the stray sheep of his flock were snoring upon their beds a mile and a half away.

Another favourite subject was the supreme rightness of the social order as it then existed. God, in His infinite wisdom, had appointed a place for every man, woman, and child on this earth and it was their bounden duty to remain contentedly in their niches. A gentleman might seem to some of his listeners to have a pleasant, easy life, compared to theirs at field labour; but he had his duties and responsibilities, which would be far beyond their capabilities. He had to pay taxes, sit on the Bench of Magistrates, oversee his estate, and keep up his position by entertaining. Could they do these things? No. Of course they could not; and he did not suppose that a gentleman could cut as straight a furrow or mow or thatch a rick as expertly as they could. So let them be thankful and rejoice in their physical strength and the bounty of the farmer, who found them work on his land and paid them wages with his money. . . .

Some of them went to church to show off their

best clothes and to see and criticize those of their
neighbours; some because they loved to hear their
own voices raised in the hymns, or because churchgoing qualified them for the Christmas blankets
and coals; and a few to worship. There was at least
one saint and mystic in that parish and there were
several good Christian men and women, but the
majority regarded religion as something proper to extreme old
age, for which they themselves had as yet no use. . . .

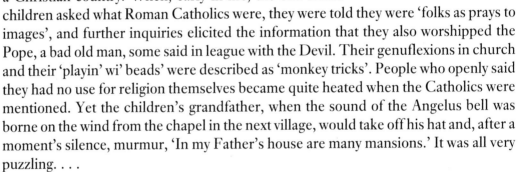

The Catholic minority at the inn was treated with respect, for a
landlord could do no wrong, especially the landlord of a
free house where such excellent beer was on tap. On
Catholicism at large, the Lark Rise people looked with
contemptuous intolerance, for they regarded it as a kind
of heathenism, and what excuse could there be for that in
a Christian country? When, early in life, the end house
children asked what Roman Catholics were, they were told they were 'folks as prays to
images', and further inquiries elicited the information that they also worshipped the
Pope, a bad old man, some said in league with the Devil. Their genuflexions in church
and their 'playin' wi' beads' were described as 'monkey tricks'. People who openly said
they had no use for religion themselves became quite heated when the Catholics were
mentioned. Yet the children's grandfather, when the sound of the Angelus bell was
borne on the wind from the chapel in the next village, would take off his hat and, after a
moment's silence, murmur, 'In my Father's house are many mansions.' It was all very
puzzling. . . .

The Methodists were a class apart. Provided they did not attempt to convert others,
religion in them was tolerated. Every Sunday evening they held a service in one of their
cottages, and, whenever she could obtain permission at home, it was Laura's delight to
attend. This was not because the service appealed to her; she really preferred the
church service; but because Sunday evening at home was a trying time, with the whole
family huddled round the fire and Father reading and no one allowed to speak and
barely to move.

Permission was hard to get, for her father did not approve of 'the ranters'; nor did he
like Laura to be out after dark. But one time out of four or five when she asked, he
would grunt and nod, and she would dash off before her mother could raise any
objection. Sometimes Edmund would follow her, and they would seat themselves on
one of the hard, white-scrubbed benches in the meeting house, prepared to hear all
that was to be heard and see all that was to be seen.

The first thing that would have struck any one less accustomed to the place was its marvellous cleanliness. The cottage walls were whitewashed and always fresh and clean. The everyday furniture had been carried out to the barn to make way for the long white wooden benches, and before the window with its drawn white blind stood a table covered with a linen cloth, on which were the lamp, a large Bible, and a glass of water for the visiting preacher, whose seat was behind it. Only the clock and a pair of red china dogs on the mantelpiece remained to show that on other days people lived and cooked and ate in the room. A bright fire always glowed in the grate and there was a smell compounded of lavender, lamp-oil, and packed humanity. . . .

If the visiting preacher happened to be late, which he often was with a long distance to cover on foot, the host would give out a hymn from Sankey and Moody's Hymn-Book, which would be sung without musical accompaniment to one of the droning, long-drawn-out tunes peculiar to the community. At other times one of the brethren would break into extempore prayer, in the course of which he would retail the week's news so far as it affected the gathering, prefacing each statement with 'Thou knowest', or 'As thou knowest, Lord'. It amused Laura and Edmund to hear old Mr Barker telling God that it had not rained for a fortnight and that his carrot bed was getting 'mortal dry'; or that swine fever had broken out at a farm four miles away and that his own pig didn't seem 'no great shakes'; or that somebody had mangled his wrist in a turnip cutter and had come out of hospital, but found it still stiff; for, as they said to each other afterwards, God must know already, as He knew everything. But these one-sided conversations with the Deity were conducted in a spirit of simple faith. 'Cast your care upon Him' was a text they loved and took literally. To them God was a loving Father who loved to listen to His children's confidences. No trouble was too small to bring to 'the Mercy Seat'. . . .

But the chief interest centred in the travelling preacher, especially if he were a stranger who had not been there before. Would he preach the Word, or would he be one of those who rambled on for an hour or more, yet said nothing? Most of these men, who gave up their Sunday rest and walked miles to preach at the village meeting houses, were farm labourers or small shopkeepers. With a very few exceptions they were poor, uneducated men. 'The blind leading the blind,' Laura's father said of them. They may have been unenlightened in some respects, but some of them had gifts no education could have given. There was something fine about their discourses, as they raised their voices in rustic eloquence and testified to the cleansing power of 'the Blood', forgetting themselves and their own imperfections of speech in their ardour. . . .

Methodism, as known and practised there, was a poor people's religion, simple and crude; but its adherents brought to it more fervour than was shown by the church congregation, and appeared to obtain more comfort and support from it than the church could give. Their lives were exemplary.

Many in the hamlet who attended neither church nor chapel and said they had no use for religion, guided their lives by the light of a few homely precepts, such as 'Pay your way and fear nobody'; 'Right's right and wrong's no man's right'; 'Tell the truth and shame the devil', and 'Honesty is the best policy'.

Strict honesty was the policy of most of them; although there were a few who were said to 'find anything before 'tis lost' and to whom findings were keepings. Children were taught to 'Know it's a sin to steal a pin', and when they brought home some doubtful finding, saying they did not think it belonged to anybody, their mothers would say severely, 'You knowed it didn't belong to you, and what don't belong to you belongs to somebody else. So go and put it back where you found it, before I gets the stick to you.'

Liars were more detested than thieves. 'A liar did ought to have a good memory,' they would say, or, more witheringly, 'You can lock up from a thief, but you can't from a liar.' Any statement which departed in the least degree from plain fact was a lie; any one who ate a plum from an overhanging bough belonging to a neighbour's tree was a thief. It was a stark code in which black was black and white was white; there were no intermediate shades. . . .

The Rector visited each cottage in turn, working his way conscientiously round the hamlet from door to door, so that by the end of the year he had called upon everybody. When he tapped with his gold-headed cane at a cottage door there would come a sound of scuffling within, as unseemly objects were hustled out of sight, for the whisper would have gone round that he had been seen getting over the stile and his knock would have been recognized.

The women received him with respectful tolerance. A chair was dusted with an apron and the doing of housework or cooking was suspended while his hostess, seated uncomfortably on the edge of one of her own chairs, waited for him to open the conversation. When the weather had been discussed, the health of the inmates and absent children inquired about, and the progress of the pig and the prospect of the allotment crops, there came an awkward pause, during which both racked their brains to find something to talk about. There was nothing. The Rector never mentioned religion. That was looked upon in the parish as one of his chief virtues, but it limited the possible topics of conversation. Apart from his autocratic ideas, he was a kindly man, and he had come to pay a friendly call, hoping, no doubt, to get to know and to understand his parishioners better. But the gulf between them was too wide; neither he nor his hostess could bridge it. The kindly inquiries made and answered, they had

nothing more to say to each other, and, after much 'ah-ing' and 'er-ing', he would rise from his seat, and be shown out with alacrity.

His daughter visited the hamlet more frequently. Any fine afternoon she might have been seen, gathering up her long, full skirts to mount the stile and tripping daintily between the allotment plots. As a widowed clergyman's only daughter, parochial visiting was, to her, a sacred duty; but she did not come in any district-visiting spirit, to criticize household management, or give unasked advice on the bringing up of children; hers, like her father's, were intended to be friendly calls. Considering her many kindnesses to the women, she might have been expected to be more popular than she was. None of them welcomed her visits. Some would lock their doors and pretend to be out; others would rattle their teacups when they saw her coming, hoping she would say, as she sometimes did, 'I hear you are at tea, so I won't come in.'

The only spoken complaint about her was that she talked too much. 'That Miss Ellison; she'd fair talk a donkey's hind leg off,' they would say; but that was a failing they tolerated in others, and one to which they were not averse in her, once she was installed in their best chair and some item of local gossip was being discussed.

Perhaps at the root of their unease in her presence was the subconscious feeling of contrast between her lot and theirs. Her neat little figure, well corseted in; her clear, high-pitched voice, good clothes, and faint scent of lily-of-the-valley perfume put them, in their workaday garb and all blowsed from their cooking or water-fetching, at a disadvantage.

She never suspected she was unwanted. On the contrary, she was most careful to visit each cottage in rotation, lest jealousy should arise. She would inquire about every member of the family in turn, listen to extracts from letters of daughters in service, sympathize with those who had tales of woe to tell, discuss everything that had happened since her last visit, and insist upon nursing the baby the while, and only smile good-naturedly when it wetted the front of her frock.

Her last visit of the day was always to the end house, where, over a cup of tea, she would become quite confidential. She and Laura's mother were 'Miss Margaret' and 'Emma' to each other, for they had known each other from birth, including the time when Emma was nurse to Miss Margaret's young friends at the neighbouring rectory.

Laura, supposed to be deep in her book, but really all ears, learnt that, surprisingly, Miss Ellison, the great Miss Ellison, had her troubles. She had a brother, reputed 'wild', in the parish, whom her father had forbidden the house, and much of their talk was about 'my brother Robert', or 'Master Bobbie', and the length of time since his last letter, and whether he had gone to Brazil, as he had said he should, or whether he was still in London. 'What I feel, Emma, is that he is such a boy, and you know what the world is – what perils –' Then Emma's cheerful rejoinder: 'Don't you worry yourself, Miss Margaret. He can look after himself all right, Master Bob can.'

Sometimes Emma would venture to admire something Miss Margaret was wearing. 'Excuse me, Miss Margaret, but that mauve muslin really does become you'; and Miss Ellison would look pleased. She had probably few compliments, for one of her type was not likely to be admired in those days of pink and white dollishness, although her clear, healthy pallor, with only the faintest flush of pink, her broad white brow, grey eyes, and dark hair waving back to the knot at her nape were at least distinguished looking. And she could not at that time have been more than thirty, although to Laura she seemed quite old, and the hamlet women called her an old maid.

Such a life as hers must have been is almost unimaginable now. Between playing the harmonium in church, teaching in Sunday school, ordering her father's meals and overseeing the maids, she must have spent hours doing needlework. Coarse, unattractive needlework, too, cross-over shawls and flannel petticoats for the old women, flannel shirts and long, thick knitted stockings for the old men, these, as well as the babies' print frocks, were all made by her own hands. Excepting a fortnight's visit a year to relatives, the only outing she was known to have was a weekly drive to the market town, shopping, in her father's high, yellow-wheeled dogcart, with the fat fox-terrier, Beppo, panting behind. . . .

If one of the women was accused of hoarding her best clothes instead of wearing them, she would laugh and say: 'Ah! I be savin' they for high days an' holidays an' bonfire nights.' If she had, they would have lasted a long time, for there were very few holidays and scarcely any which called for a special toilet.

Christmas Day passed very quietly. The men had a holiday from work and the children from school and the churchgoers attended special Christmas services. Mothers who had young children would buy them an orange each and a handful of nuts; but, except at the end house and the inn, there was no hanging up of stockings, and those who had no kind elder sister or aunt in service to send them parcels got no

Christmas presents.

Still, they did manage to make a little festival of it. Every year the farmer killed an ox for the purpose and gave each of his men a joint of beef, which duly appeared on the Christmas dinner-table together with plum pudding – not Christmas pudding, but suet duff with a good sprinkling of raisins. Ivy and other evergreens (it was not a holly country) were hung from the ceiling and over the pictures; a bottle of home-made wine was uncorked, a good fire was made up, and, with doors and windows closed against the keen, wintry weather, they all settled down by their own firesides for a kind of super-Sunday. There was little visiting of neighbours and there were no family reunions, for the girls in service could not be spared at that season, and the few boys who had gone out in the world were mostly serving abroad in the Army.

There were still bands of mummers in some of the larger villages, and village choirs went carol-singing about the countryside; but none of these came to the hamlet, for they knew the collection to be expected there would not make it worth their while. A few families, sitting by their own firesides, would sing carols and songs; that, and more and better food and a better fire than usual, made up their Christmas cheer.

The Sunday of the Feast was more exciting. Then strangers, as well as friends, came from far and near to throng the houses and inn and to promenade on the stretch of road which ran through the hamlet. On that day the big ovens were heated and nearly every family managed to have a joint of beef and a Yorkshire pudding for dinner. The men wore their best suits, complete with collar and tie, and the women brought out their treasured finery and wore it, for, even if no relatives from a distance were expected, some one might be 'popping in', if not to dinner, to tea or supper. Half a crown, at least, had been saved from the harvest money for spending at the inn, and the jugs and beer-cans went merrily round the Rise. 'Arter all, 'tis the Feast,' they said; 'an't only comes once a year,' and they enjoyed the extra food and drink and the excitement of seeing so many people about, never dreaming that they were celebrating the dedication five hundred years before of the little old church in the mother village which so few of them attended. . . .

The Monday of the Feast – for it lasted two days – was kept by women and children only, the men being at work. It was a great day for tea parties; mothers and sisters and aunts and cousins coming in droves from about the neighbourhood. The chief delicacy at these teas was 'baker's cake', a rich, fruity, spicy dough cake, obtained in the following manner. The housewife provided all the ingredients excepting the dough, putting raisins and currants, lard, sugar, and spice in a basin which she gave to the baker, who added the dough, made and baked the cake, and returned it, beautifully browned in his big oven. The charge was the same as that for a loaf of bread the same size, and the result was delicious. 'There's only one fault wi' these 'ere baker's cakes,' the women used to say; 'they won't keep!' And they would not; they were too good and there were too many children about.

The women made their houses very clean and neat for Feast Monday, and, with hollyhocks nodding in at the open windows and a sight of the clean, yellow stubble of the cleared fields beyond, and the hum of friendly talk and laughter within, the tea parties were very pleasant. . . .

Harvest time was a natural holiday. 'A hemmed hard-worked 'un,' the men would have said; but they all enjoyed the stir and excitement of getting in the crops and their own importance as skilled and trusted workers, with extra beer at the farmer's expense

and extra harvest money to follow.

The 'eighties brought a succession of hot summers and, day after day, as harvest time approached, the children at the end house would wake to the dewy, pearly pink of a fine summer dawn and the *swizzh, swizzh* of the early morning breeze rustling through the ripe corn beyond their doorstep.

Then, very early one morning, the men would come out of their houses, pulling on coats and lighting pipes as they hurried and calling to each other with skyward glances: 'Think weather's a-gooin' to hold?' For three weeks or more during harvest the hamlet was astir before dawn and the homely odours of bacon frying, wood fires and tobacco smoke overpowered the pure, damp, earthy scent of the fields. It would be school holidays then and the children at the end house always wanted to get up hours before their time. . . .

Against the billowing gold of the fields the hedges stood dark, solid and dewsleeked; dewdrops beaded the gossamer webs, and the children's feet left long, dark trails on the dewy turf. There were night scents of wheat-straw and flowers and moist earth on the air and the sky was fleeced with pink clouds.

For a few days or a week or a fortnight, the fields stood 'ripe unto harvest'. It was the one perfect period in the hamlet year. The human eye loves to rest upon wide expanses of pure colour: the moors in the purple heyday of the heather, miles of green downland, and the sea when it lies calm and blue and boundless, all delight it; but to some none of these, lovely though they all are, can give the same satisfaction of spirit as acres upon acres of golden corn. *There* is both beauty and bread and the seeds of bread for future generations. . . .

In the fields where the harvest had begun all was bustle and activity. At that time the mechanical reaper with long, red, revolving arms like windmill sails had already

appeared in the locality; but it was looked upon by the men as an auxiliary, a farmers' toy; the scythe still did most of the work and they did not dream it would ever be superseded. So while the red sails revolved in one field and the youth on the driver's seat of the machine called cheerily to his horses and women followed behind to bind the corn into sheaves, in the next field a band of men would be whetting their scythes and mowing by hand as their fathers had done before them.

With no idea that they were at the end of a long tradition, they still kept up the old country custom of choosing as their leader the tallest and most highly skilled man amongst them, who was then called 'King of the Mowers'. For several harvests in the 'eighties they were led by the man known as Boamer. He had served in the Army and was still a fine, well-set-up young fellow with flashing white teeth and a skin darkened by fiercer than English suns.

With a wreath of poppies and green bindweed trails around his wide, rush-plaited hat, he led the band down the swathes as they mowed and decreed when and for how long they should halt for 'a breather' and what drinks should be had from the yellow stone jar they kept under the hedge in a shady corner of the field. They did not rest often or long; for every morning they set themselves to accomplish an amount of work in the day that they knew would tax all their powers till long after sunset. 'Set yourself more than you can do and you'll do it' was one of their maxims, and some of their feats in the harvest field astonished themselves as well as the onlooker.

Old Monday, the bailiff, went riding from field to field on his long-tailed, grey pony. Not at that season to criticize, but rather to encourage, and to carry strung to his saddle the hooped and handled miniature barrel of beer provided by the farmer.

One of the smaller fields was always reserved for any of the women who cared to go reaping. Formerly all the able-bodied women not otherwise occupied had gone as a matter of course; but, by the 'eighties, there were only three or four, beside the regular field women, who could hand the sickle. Often the Irish harvesters had to be called in to finish the field. . . .

After the mowing and reaping and binding came the carrying, the busiest time of all. Every man and boy put his best foot forward then, for, when the corn was cut and dried it was imperative to get it stacked and thatched before the weather broke. All day and far into the twilight the yellow-and-blue painted farm wagons passed and repassed along the roads between the field and the stack-yard. Big cart-horses returning with an empty wagon were made to gallop like two-year-olds. Straws hung on the roadside hedges and many a gate-post was knocked down through hasty driving. In the fields men pitchforked the sheaves to the one who was building the load on the wagon, and the air resounded with *Hold tights* and *Wert ups* and *Who-o-oas*. . . .

At last, in the cool dusk of an August evening, the last load was brought in, with a nest of merry boys' faces among the sheaves on the top, and the men walking alongside with pitchforks on shoulders. As they passed along the roads they shouted:

Harvest home! Harvest home!
Merry, merry, merry harvest home!

and women came to their cottage gates and waved, and the few passers-by looked up and smiled their congratulations. The joy and pleasure of the labourers in their task well done was pathetic, considering their very small share in the gain. But it was genuine enough; for they still loved the soil and rejoiced in their own work and skill in bringing forth the fruits of the soil, and harvest home put the crown on their year's work. . . .

On the morning of the harvest home dinner everybody

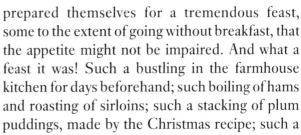

prepared themselves for a tremendous feast, some to the extent of going without breakfast, that the appetite might not be impaired. And what a feast it was! Such a bustling in the farmhouse kitchen for days beforehand; such boiling of hams and roasting of sirloins; such a stacking of plum puddings, made by the Christmas recipe; such a tapping of eighteen-gallon casks and baking of plum loaves would astonish those accustomed to the appetites of today. By noon the whole parish had assembled, the workers and their wives and children to feast and the sprinkling of the better-to-do to help with the serving. The only ones absent were the aged bedridden and their attendants, and to them, the next day, portions, carefully graded in daintiness according to their social standing, were carried by the children from the remnants of the feast. A plum pudding was considered a delicate compliment to an equal of the farmer; slices of beef or ham went to the 'bettermost poor'; and a ham-bone with plenty of meat left upon it or part of a pudding or a can of soup to the commonalty.

Long tables were laid out of doors in the shade of a barn, and soon after twelve o'clock the cottagers sat down to the good cheer, with the farmer carving at the principal table, his wife with her tea urn at another, the daughters of the house and their friends circling the tables with vegetable dishes and beer jugs, and the grandchildren, in their stiff, white, embroidered frocks, dashing hither and thither to see that everybody had what they required. As a background there was the rick-yard with its new yellow stacks and, over all, the mellow sunshine of late summer.

Passers-by on the road stopped their gigs and high dog-carts to wave greetings and shout congratulations on the weather. If a tramp looked wistfully in, he was beckoned to a seat on the straw beneath a rick and a full plate was placed on his knees. It was a picture of plenty and goodwill.

It did not do to look beneath the surface. Laura's father, who did not come into the picture, being a 'tradesman' and so not invited, used to say that the farmer paid his men starvation wages all the year and thought he made it up to them by giving that one good meal. The farmer did not think so, because he did not think at all, and the men did not think either on that day; they were too busy enjoying the food and the fun.

After the dinner there were sports and games, then dancing in the home paddock until twilight, and when, at the end of the day, the farmer, carving indoors for the family supper, paused with knife poised to listen to the last distant 'Hooray!' and exclaimed, 'A lot of good chaps! A lot of good chaps, God bless 'em!' both he and the cheering men were sincere, however mistaken.

But these modest festivals which had figured every year in everybody's life for generations were eclipsed in 1887 by Queen Victoria's Golden Jubilee.

Up to the middle of the 'eighties the hamlet had taken little interest in the Royal House. The Queen and the Prince and Princess of Wales were sometimes mentioned, but with little respect and no affection. 'The old Queen', as she was called, was supposed to have shut herself up in Balmoral Castle with a favourite servant named John Brown and to have refused to open Parliament when Mr Gladstone begged her to. The Prince was said to be leading a gay life, and the dear, beautiful Princess, afterwards Queen Alexandra, was celebrated only for her supposed make-up.

By the middle of the decade a new spirit was abroad and had percolated to the hamlet. The Queen, it appeared, had reigned fifty years. She had been a good queen, a wonderful queen, she was soon to celebrate her Jubilee, and, still more exciting, they were going to celebrate it, too, for there was going to be a big 'do' in which three villages would join for tea and sports and dancing and fireworks in the park of a local magnate. Nothing like it had ever been known before.

As the time drew nearer, the Queen and her Jubilee became the chief topic of conversation. The tradesmen gave lovely coloured portraits of her in her crown and garter ribbon on their almanacks, most of which were framed at home and hung up in the cottages. Jam could be bought in glass jugs adorned with her profile in hobnails and inscribed '1837 to 1887. Victoria the Good', and, underneath, the national catchword of the moment: 'Peace and Plenty'. The newspapers were full of the great achievements of her reign: railway travel, the telegraph, Free Trade, exports, progress, prosperity, Peace: all these blessings, it appeared, were due to her inspiration. . . .

The great day dawned at last and most of the hamlet people were up in time to see the sun burst in dazzling splendour from the pearly pink east and mount into a sky unflecked by the smallest cloud. Queen's weather indeed! And as the day began it continued. It was very hot; but nobody minded that, for the best hats could be worn without fear of showers, and those who had sunshades put by for just such an occasion could bring them forth in all their glory of deep lace or long, knotted, silk fringe.

By noon all the hamlet children had been scrubbed with soap and water and arrayed in their best clothes. 'Every bit clean, right through to the skin,' as their mothers proudly declared. Then, after a snack, calculated to sustain the family during the walk to the park, but not to spoil the appetite for tea, the mothers went upstairs to take out their own curl papers and don their best clothes. A strong scent of camphor and lavender and closely shut boxes pervaded the atmosphere around them for the rest of the day. The colours and styles did not harmonize too well with the midsummer country scene, and many might have preferred to see them in print frocks and sunbonnets; but they dressed to please themselves, not to please the artistic taste of others, and they were all the happier for it. . . .

There were more people in the park than the children had ever seen together, and the roundabouts, swings, and coconut shies were doing a roaring trade. Tea was partaken of in a huge marquee in relays, one parish at a time, and the sound of the brass band, roundabout hurdy-gurdy, coconut thwacks, and showmen's shouting surged round the frail, canvas walls like a roaring sea.

Within, the mingled scents of hot tea, dough cake, tobacco smoke, and trampled grass lent a holiday savour to a simple menu. But if the provisions were simple in quality, the quantity was prodigious. Clothes baskets of bread and butter and jam cut in thick slices and watering cans of tea, already milked and sugared, were handed round and disappeared in a twinkling. 'God bless my soul,' one old clergyman exclaimed. 'Where on earth do they put it all!' They put three-fourths of it in the same handy receptacle he himself used for his four-course dinners; but the fourth part went into their pockets. That was their little weakness – not to be satisfied with a bellyful, but to manage somehow to secure a portion to take home for next day.

After tea there were sports, with races, high jumps, dipping heads into tubs of water to retrieve sixpences with the teeth, grinning through horse-collars, the prize going to the one making the most grotesque face, and, to crown all, climbing the greased pole for the prize leg of mutton. This was a tough job, as the pole was as tall and slender as a telephone post and extremely slippery. Prudent wives would not allow their husbands to attempt it on account of spoiling their clothes, so the competition was left to the ragamuffins and a few experts who had had the foresight to bring with them a pair of old trousers. This competition must have run concurrently with the other events, for all the afternoon there was a crowd around it, and first one, then another, would 'have a go'. It was painful to watch the climbers, shinning up a few inches, then slipping back again, and, as one retired, another taking his place, until, late in the afternoon, the champion arrived, climbed slowly but steadily to the top and threw down the joint, which, by the way, must have been already roasted after four or five hours in the

139

burning sun. It was whispered around that he had carried a bag of ashes and sprinkled them on the greasy surface as he ascended.

The local gentlepeople promenaded the ground in parties: stout, red-faced squires, raising their straw hats to mop their foreheads; hunting ladies, incongruously garbed in silks and ostrich-feather boas; young girls in embroidered white muslin and boys in Eton suits. They had kind words for everybody, especially for the poor and lonely, and, from time to time, they would pause before some sight and try to enter into the spirit of the other beholders; but everywhere their arrival hushed the mirth, and there was a sigh of relief when they moved on. After dancing the first dance they disappeared, and 'now we can have some fun', the people said.

All this time Edmund and Laura, with about two hundred other children, had been let loose in the crowd to spend their pennies and watch the fun. They rode on the

wooden horses, swung in the swing-boats, pried around coconut shies and shooting booths munching coconut or rock or long strips of black liquorice, until their hands were sticky and their faces grimed.

Laura, who hated crowds and noise, was soon tired of it and looked longingly at the shady trees and woods and spinneys around the big open space where the fair was held. But before she escaped a new and wonderful experience awaited her. Before one of the booths a man was beating a drum and before him two girls were posturing and pirouetting. 'Walk up! Walk up!' he was shouting. 'Walk up and see the tightrope dancing! Only one penny admission. Walk up! Walk up!' Laura paid her penny and walked up, as did about a dozen others, the man and girls came inside, the flap of the tent was drawn, and the show began.

Laura had never heard of tightrope dancing before and she was not sure she was not dreaming it then. The outer tumult beat against the frail walls of the tent, but within was a magic circle of quiet. As she crossed to take her place with the other spectators, her feet sank deep into sawdust; and, in the subdued light which filtered through the canvas, the broad, white, pock-marked face of the man in his faded red satin and the tinsel crowns and tights of the girls seemed as unreal as a dream.

The girl who did the tightrope dancing was a fair, delicate-looking child with grey eyes and fat, pale-brown ringlets, a great contrast to her dark, bouncing gipsy-looking sister, and when she mounted to the rope stretched between two poles and did a few dance steps as she swayed gracefully along it, Laura gazed and gazed, speechless with admiration. To the simple country-bred child the performance was marvellous. It came to an end all too soon for her; for not much could be done to entertain a house which only brought a shilling or so to the box office; but the impression remained with her as a glimpse into a new and fascinating world. There were few five-barred gates in

the vicinity of Laura's home on which she did not attempt a little pirouetting along the top bar during the next year or two.

The tightrope dancing was her outstanding memory of the great Queen's Jubilee; but the merrymaking went on for hours after that. All the way home in the twilight, the end house party could hear the popping of fireworks behind them and, turning, see rockets and showers of golden rain above the dark tree-tops. At last, standing at their own garden gate, they heard the roaring of cheers from hundreds of throats and the band playing 'God save the Queen'.

They were first home and the hamlet was in darkness, but the twilight was luminous over the fields and the sky right round to the north was still faintly pink. A cat rubbed itself against their legs and mewed; the pig in the sty woke and grunted a protest against the long day's neglect. A light breeze rustled through the green corn and shivered the garden bushes, releasing the scent of stocks and roses and sunbaked grass and the grosser smells of cabbage beds and pigsties. It had been a great day – the greatest day they were ever likely to see, however long they lived, they were told; but it was over and they were home and home was best.

After the Jubilee nothing ever seemed quite the same. The old Rector died and the farmer, who had seemed immovable excepting by death, had to retire to make way for the heir of the landowning nobleman who intended to farm the family estates himself. He brought with him the new self-binding reaping machine and women were no longer required in the harvest field. At the hamlet several new brides took possession of houses previously occupied by elderly people and brought new ideas into the place. The last of the bustles disappeared and leg-o'-mutton sleeves were 'all the go'. The new Rector's wife took her Mothers' Meeting women for a trip to London. Babies were christened new names; Wanda was one, Gwendolin another. The innkeeper's wife got in cases of tinned salmon and Australian rabbit. The Sanitary Inspector appeared for the first time at the hamlet and shook his head over the pigsties and privies. Wages rose, prices soared, and new needs multiplied. People began to speak of 'before the Jubilee' much as we in the nineteen-twenties spoke of 'before the war', either as a golden time or as one of exploded ideas, according to the age of the speaker.

And all the time boys were being born or growing up in the parish, expecting to follow the plough all their lives, or, at most, to do a little mild soldiering or go to work in a town. Gallipoli? Kut? Vimy Ridge? Ypres? What did they know of such places? but they were to know them, and when the time came they did not flinch. Eleven out of that tiny community never came back again. A brass plate on the wall of the church immediately over the old end house seat is engraved with their names. A double column, five names long, then, last and alone, the name of Edmund.

OVER TO CANDLEFORD

——— VII ———
'A BIT OF A TELL'

'COME the summer, we'll borrow old Polly and the spring cart from the "Wagon and Horses" and all go over to Candleford,' their father said, for the ten-millionth time, thought Laura. Although he had said it so often they had never been. They had not been anywhere farther than the market town for the Saturday shopping.

Once, when some one asked them how long they had lived in their cottage, Laura had replied, 'Oh, for years and years,' and Edmund had said 'Always'; but his always was only five years and her years and years were barely seven. That was why, when their mother told them that the greatest mistake in life is to be born poor, they did not realize that they themselves had made that initial blunder. They were too young and had no means of comparison. . . .

Candleford was a wonderful place. Her mother said there were rows of shops there, simply stuffed with toys and sweets and furs and muffs and watches and chains and other delightful things. 'You should see them at Christmas,' she said, 'all lit up like a fair. All you want then is a purseful of money!' The Candleford people had pursefuls of money, for wages were higher there, and they had gas to light them to bed and drew their water out of taps, instead of up from a well. She had heard her parents say so. 'What he wants is a job at some place such as Candleford,' her father would say of some promising boy. 'He'd do himself some good there. Here, there's nothing.' This surprised Laura, for she had thought there were many exciting things about the hamlet. 'Is there a brook there?' she asked, rather hoping there was not, and she was told there was a river, which was wider than any brook and had a stone bridge, instead of a rickety old plank to cross by. A magnificent place, indeed, and she hoped soon to see it. 'Come the summer' her father had said, but the summer had come and gone again and nothing more had been said about borrowing Polly and the spring cart. Then, always, something or other happened to push the idea of Candleford to the back of her mind. One dreary November the pigs were ill. They refused to eat and became so weak they had to lean against the rails of their sties for support. Some of them died and were buried in quicklime, which was said to burn up their bodies in no time. Horrible thought to be dead and buried in quicklime and soon nothing left of what had been so much alive! Her mother said it was a far worse thought that the poor people had lost their pigs, after paying for their food all those months, too, and when their own

pigs were killed – both had escaped – she was more than usually generous with the plates of liver and fat and other oddments always sent to neighbours as a compliment. Many of the people who had lost their pigs still owed for the food. They had depended upon being able to pay for that in kind when the animal was fattened. One man took to poaching and was caught and sent to prison, then every one had to take half loaves and small screws of tea and sugar to help his wife to keep the home going, until the whisper went round that she had three different lots of butter in the house, given by different people to whom she had pleaded poverty, and that the J.P. himself had sent a sovereign. People looked sourly upon her after that was known, and said, 'Crime seems to pay nowadays.'

Sometimes, instead of saying. 'Here there's nothing,' her father would say, 'Here there's nobody,' meaning nobody he thought worth considering. But Laura never tired of considering the hamlet neighbours, and, as she grew older, would listen to, and piece together, the things they said until she had learned quite a lot from them. She liked the older women best such as Old Queenie, Old Sally, and Old Mrs Prout, old countrywomen who still wore sun-bonnets and stayed in their own homes and gardens and cared not at all about what was in fashion and very little for gossip. They said they did not hold with gadding about from house to house. Queenie had her lace-making and her beehives to watch; Old Sally her brewing and her bacon to cure; if anybody wanted to see them, they knew where to find them. 'Crusty old dames,' some of the younger women called them, especially when one of them had refused to lend them something. To Laura they seemed like rocks, keeping firm in their places, while those about them drifted around, always on the look-out for some new sensation. But only a few were left who kept to the old country ways, and the other women were interesting, too. Although they wore much the same kind of clothes and lived in similar houses, no two of them

were really alike.

In theory all the hamlet women were on friendly terms with each other, at least as far as 'passing the time of day' when they met, for they had an almost morbid dread of giving offence and would go out of their way to be pleasant to other women they would rather not have seen. As Laura's mother said: 'You can't *afford* to be on bad terms with anybody in a small place like this.' But in that, as in more sophisticated societies, there was a tendency to form sets. The members of the slightly more prosperous of these, consisting mostly of the newly married and those of the older women whose children were grown up and off their hands, would change into a clean apron in the afternoon and stay quietly at home, sewing or ironing, or put on their hats and go out to call upon their friends, carefully knocking at the door before they lifted the latch. The commoner kind burst hatless into their neighbour's houses to borrow something or to relate some breathless item of news, or they would spend the afternoon shouting it across gardens or from doorsteps, or hold long, bantering conversations with the baker, or the oilman, or any one else who happened to call and found themselves unable to get away without downright rudeness.

Laura's mother belonged to the first category and those who came to her house were mostly her own special friends. They had a few other callers, however, and those Laura thought far more interesting than young Mrs Massey, who was always making baby's clothes, although at that time she had no baby (Laura thought afterwards, when a baby arrived for her, it was a lucky coincidence), or Mrs Hadley, who was always talking about her daughter in service, or Mrs Finch, who was 'not too strong' and had to be given the best seat, nearest the fire. The only interesting thing about her was the little blue bottle of smelling-salts she carried, and that ceased to interest after she had handed it to Laura, telling her to give a good sniff, then laughed when the tears ran down her cheeks. Not at all Laura's idea of a joke!

She liked Rachel much better. Although never invited, she would drift in sometimes, 'just to have a tell', as she expressed it. Her 'tells' were worth hearing, for she knew everything that happened, 'and a good lot more, too', her enemies said. 'Ask Rachel,' some one would say with a shrug if the whole of the facts of a happening were not known, and Rachel, when appealed to, if she, too, were not quite sure, would say in her loud, hearty voice, 'Well to tell the truth, I haven't ever quite got to the bottom of that business. But I 'ull know, that I 'ull, for I'll go to th' fountain-head and ax.' And off she would march with all the good-natured effrontery imaginable to ask Mrs Beaby if it was 'a fac'' that her young Em was leaving her place before her year was up, or Charley's mother if it was true that he and Nell had quarrelled coming home from church last Sunday, and had they made it up, or were they still 'off at hooks', as they called an estrange-ment.

When Rachel dropped in for a tell, others were sure to follow. Laura, lying on her stomach on the hearth-rug with a picture book propped up before her, or cutting out patterns from paper in a corner, would hear their voices rising and falling or dropping to a whisper when some item they were discussing was not considered suitable for children's ears. She would sometimes long to ask questions, but dare not, for it was a strict rule there that children should be seen, but not heard. It was better not even to laugh when something funny was said, for that might call attention to oneself and some one might say: 'That child's gettin' too knowin'. I hope she ain't goin' to turn out one of them forrard sort, for I can't abide 'em.' At that her mother would bridle and say that, far from being forward, she was rather young for her age, and as to being knowing, she

didn't suppose she had heard what was said, but had laughed because they were laughing. At the same time, she took care to send Laura upstairs, or out into the garden for something, when she thought the conversation was taking an unsuitable turn.

Sometimes one of them would let fall a remark about the vague far-distant days before the children were born. 'My ole gran-fer used to say that all the land between here and the church wer' left by will to th' poor o' th' parish in the old times; all common land of turf and fuzz 'twas then; but 'twer' all stole away an' cut up into fields,' and another would agree, 'Yes, so I've allus heard.'

Sometimes one of them would bring out some surprising saying, as Patty Wardup did when the rest of the company were discussing Mrs Eames's fur cape: she couldn't have bought it and it certainly did not grow upon her back, yet she had appeared in it last Sunday at church, and not so much as a word to anybody as to how she had got it. True, as Mrs Baker suggested, it did look something like a coachman's shoulder tippet

– dark, thick fur, bearskin, they called it – and she had once said she had a brother who was a coachman somewhere up country. Then Patty, who had been pensively twisting her doorkey between her fingers and taking no part in the conversation, said quietly: 'The golden ball rolls to everybody's feet once in a lifetime. That's what my Uncle Jarvis used to say and I've seen it myself, over and over.'

What golden ball? And who was her Uncle Jarvis? And what had a golden ball to do with Mrs Eames's fur tippet? No wonder they all laughed and said, 'She's dreaming as usual!' . . .

Then there was a young married woman named Gertie who passed as a beauty, entirely on the strength of a tiny waist and simpering smile. She was a great reader of novelettes and had romantic ideas. Before her marriage she had been a housemaid at one of the country mansions where men-servants were kept, and their company and

compliments had spoiled her for her kind, honest great cart-horse of a husband. She loved to talk about her conquests, telling of the time Mr Pratt, the butler, had danced with her four times at the servants' ball, and how jealous her John had been. He had been invited for her sake but could not dance, and had sat there all the evening, like a great gowk, in his light-grey Sunday suit, with his great red hands hanging down between his knees, and a chrysanthemum in his buttonhole as big as a pancake.

She had worn her white silk, the one she was afterwards married in, and her hair had been curled by a real hairdresser – the maids had clubbed together to pay for his attendance, and he had afterwards stayed for the dancing and paid special attention to Gertrude. 'And you should've seen our John, his eyes simply rolling with jealousy . . .' But, if she managed to get so far, she was then interrupted. No one wanted to hear about her conquests, but they were willing to hear about the dresses. What did the cook wear? Black lace over a red silk underslip. That sounded handsome. And the head housemaid and the stillroom maid, and so on, down to the tweeny, who, it had to be confessed, could afford nothing more exciting than her best frock of grey cloth.

Gertie was the only one of them all who discussed her relations with her husband. 'I don't think our Johnny loves me any more,' she would sigh, 'He went off to work this morning without kissing me.' Or, 'Our John's getting a regular chaw-bacon. He went to sleep and snored in his chair after tea last night. I felt that lonely I could have cried me eyes out.' And the more robust characters would laugh and ask her what more she expected of a man who had been at work in the fields all day, or say, 'Times is changed, my gal. You ain't courtin' no longer.'. . .

Laura did not like Gertie's face. Her features were not bad, but she had protruding pale blue eyes of which the whites were always faintly bloodshot, and her complexion was of a sickly yellowish shade. Even her small mouth, so much admired by some of the

hamlet judges of beauty, was repulsive to a child. It was drawn up so close that the lips made tiny wrinkles, like stitches round a buttonhole. 'A mouth like a hen's backside', one rude man said of it. . . .

The hamlet people's attitude towards those they called 'the gentry' was peculiar. They took a pride in their rich and powerful country-house neighbours, especially when titled. The old Earl in the next parish was spoken of as 'our Earl' and when the flag, flown from the tower of his mansion to show he was in residence, could be seen floating above tree-tops they would say: 'I see our family's at home again.'

They sometimes saw him pass through the hamlet in his carriage, an old, old man, sunk deep in cushions and half-buried in rugs, often too comatose to be aware of, or acknowledge, their curtsies. He had never spoken to them or given them anything, for they did not live in his cottages, and in the way of Christmas coals and blankets he had his own parish to attend to; but the men worked on his land, though not directly

employed by him, and by some inherited instinct they felt he belonged to them. . . .

Landowners of established rank and stern or kindly JPs and their ladies were respected. Some of the sons or grandsons of local families were said to be 'wild young devils' and were looked upon with a kind of horrified admiration. The tradition of the Hell-Fire Club had not entirely faded, and one young nobleman was reputed to have 'gambled away' one of his family estates at one sitting. There were hints of more lurid orgies in which a bunch of good-looking country girls were supposed to figure, and a saintly curate, an old white-haired man, went to admonish the young spark, at that time living alone in a wing of the otherwise deserted family mansion. There was no record of the conversation, but the result was known. The older man was pushed or kicked down the front door flight of steps and the door was banged and bolted against him. Then, the story went, he raised himself to his knees and prayed aloud for 'the poor sinful child' within. The gardener, greatly daring, supported him to his cottage and made him rest before attempting to walk home.

But the great majority of the country gentlepeople lived decent, if, according to hamlet standards, not particularly useful lives. In summer the carriage was at the door at three o'clock in the afternoon to take the lady of the house and her grown-up daughters, if any, to pay calls. If they found no one in, they left cards, turned down at the corner, or not turned down, according to etiquette. Or they stayed at home to receive their own callers and played croquet and drank tea under spreading cedars on exquisitely kept lawns. In winter they hunted with the local pack; and, summer and winter, they never failed to attend Sunday morning service at their parish church. They had always a smile and a nod for their poorer neighbours who saluted them, with more substantial favours for those who lived in the cottages on their estates. As to their inner lives, the commonalty knew no more than the Britons knew of the Romans who inhabited the villas dotted about the countryside; and it is doubtful if the county families knew more of their poorer neighbours than the Romans did of theirs, in spite of speaking the same language.

Here and there the barrier of caste was overstepped. Perhaps by some young man or girl who, in advance of their time, realized that the population beyond their park gates were less 'the poor' in a lump than individual men and women who happened to have been born to poverty. Of such it was sometimes said: 'He's different, Master Raymond is;

you can say anything to him, he's more like one of ourselves than one of the gentry. Makes you split your sides, he does, with some of his tales, and he's got a feeling heart, too, and don't button his pockets too tight. Good thing if there were more like him.' Or: 'Miss Dorothy, now, she's different. No asking questions and questions when she comes to see anybody; but she sets her down and if you've a mind to tell her anything, you can and know it won't go no further. I udn't mind seeing her come in when I was in the godspeed of washday, and that's saying something.'

On the other hand, there were old nurses and trusted maids who had come to be regarded as individuals and loved as true friends, irrespective of class, by those they served. And the name of 'friend', when applied to them in words, gave them a deeper satisfaction than any material benefit. A retired lady's maid, whom Laura knew later, spoke to her many times with much feeling of what she evidently regarded as the crown of her experiences. She had been for many years maid to a titled lady moving in high society, had dressed her for royal courts, undressed and put her to bed in illness, travelled with her, indulged her innocent vanities, and knew, for she could not help knowing, being so near her person, her most intimate griefs. At last 'Her Ladyship', grown old, lay upon her deathbed and her maid, who was helping to nurse her, happened to be alone in the room with her, her relatives, none of whom were very near ones, being downstairs at dinner. ' "Raise me up," she said, and I raised her up, and when she put her arms round my neck to help lift her, she kissed me and said, "*My friend*," ' and Miss Wilson, twenty years after, considered that kiss and those two words a more ample reward for her years of devotion than the nice cottage and annuity she received under the will of the poor lady. . . .

— VIII —

OVER TO CANDLEFORD

VERY early one Sunday morning, while the rest of the hamlet was still asleep and the sky was still pink and the garden flowers and currant bushes were still greyish-rough with dew, they heard the sounds of wheels drawing up at their gate and knew that the innkeeper's old pony had come with the spring cart to take them.

Father and Mother rode on the front seat, Father in his best black coat and grey-striped trousers and Mother resplendent in her pale grey wedding gown with rows and rows of narrow blue velvet ribbon edging its many flounces. The wedding bonnet had long been cast aside, for, as she often said, 'headgear does date so', and on this occasion she wore a tiny blue velvet bonnet, like a little flat mat on her hair, with wide velvet strings tied in a bow under her chin, – a new bonnet, the procuring of which had helped to delay the expedition. Upon her lap she nursed a basket containing the presents; a bottle of her elderberry wine, a fowl she had specially fattened, and a length of pillow-lace, made to order by a neighbour, which she thought would make nice neckfrills for the cousins' best frocks. Their father, not to be outdone in generosity, at the last moment filled the back of the cart, where Edmund and Laura were to sit, with a selection of his choicest vegetables, so that, throughout the drive, Laura's legs rested higher than her seat on a sack of spring cabbage, the first of the season.

At last the children were strapped into the high, narrow seat with their backs to those of their parents and off they went, their father coaxing the old grey mare past her stable door, which she made determined efforts to enter, with: 'Come on, Polly, old girl. Not tired already. Why, we haven't started yet.' Later on, he lost patience and called her 'a measley old screw', and once, when she stopped dead in the middle of the road, he said, 'Damn the mare!' and their mother looked back over the shoulder as though she feared the animal's owner might hear. Between the stops, she trotted in little bursts, and the children bumped up and down in their seat like rubber balls bouncing. All of which was as exciting to them as a flight in an aeroplane would be to a

153

modern child. . . .

'Pat, pat, pat', went Polly's hooves in the dust, 'creak, creak, creak', went the harness, and 'rattle, rattle, rattle', went the iron-tyred wheels over the stony places. The road might have been made entirely for their convenience. There was no other vehicle upon it. The farm carts and bakers' vans which passed that way on week-days were standing in yards with their shafts pointing skyward; the gentry's carriages reposed in lofty, stone-paved coach-houses, and coachmen and carters and drivers were all still in bed, for it was Sunday.

The blinds of roadside cottages were drawn and their gardens were deserted of all but a prowling cat or a thrush cracking a snail on a stone, and the children bumped and jolted on through this early morning world with their hearts full of blissful expectation.

They were going over to Candleford. It was always called 'going over', for the country people never spoke of just plain going anywhere; it had to be going up or down or round or over to a place, and there were so many ups and downs, so many small streams to cross and so many gates across roads to open between their home and Candleford that 'going over' seemed best to describe the journey.

Towards midday they passed through a village where the people, in their Sunday best, were streaming towards the lychgate of the church. The squire and the farmers wore top hats, and the squire's head gardener and the schoolmaster and the village carpenter. The farm labourers wore bowlers, or, the older men, soft, round black felts. With the top-hatted men were women in rich, dark, heavy dresses who clung to their husband's arms while their children walked meekly in front or, not so meekly, behind them. Other villagers in work-day clothes, with very clean shirts and their boots unlaced for greater Sunday ease, carried their dinners to the baker's, or stood in a group at the bakehouse door; while slowly up and down the road in front of them paced a handsome pair of greys with a carriage behind them and a coachman and a footman on the box with cockades in their glossy hats. Shepherded by their teachers, the school-children marched two and two to church from the Sunday School. . . .

Soon after that Candleford came out to meet them. First, wayside cottages embowered in flower gardens, then cottages in pairs with iron railings enclosing neat little front plots and tiled paths leading up to the doors. Then the gasometer (for they actually had gas at Candleford!) and the railway station, which made the town accessible to all but such cross-country districts as theirs. Then came pavements and lamp-posts and people, more people than they had ever seen together in their lives before. But, while they were still on the outskirts, they felt their mother nudge their father's arm and heard her ejaculate: 'There's pomp for you! Feathers, if you please!' Then, throwing her voice ahead: 'Why, it's Ethel and Alma, coming to meet us. Here are your cousins. Turn round and wave to them, dears!' Still held by the strap, Laura wriggled round and saw, coming towards them, two tall girls in white. . . .

'So this is Laura? And this is dear little Edmund? How do you do? How do you do, dear?' Alma was twelve and Ethel thirteen, but their cool, grown-up manner might have belonged to twenty-five and thirty. Laura began to wish herself back at home as, one blush of embarrassment all over, she answered for herself and Edmund. She could scarcely believe that these two tall, well-dressed, nearly grown-up girls were her cousins. She had expected something quite different.

However, things were easier when their equipage moved on, with Ethel and Alma holding on, one on each side of the tail board, and smiling a little as they answered their uncle's shouted questions. 'Yes, Uncle,' Alma was still at the Candleford school; but Ethel was at Miss Bussell's, a weekly boarder; she came home on Friday night and went back on Monday morning. She was going to stay there until she was old enough to go to the Training College for Schoolteachers. 'That's right!' called Laura's father. 'Stuff your own brains now and you'll be able to stuff other people's hereafter. And Alma, is she going to be a teacher, too?' Oh, no, when she left school she was going to be apprenticed to a Court dressmaker in Oxford. 'That's first rate,' said their uncle. 'Then when Laura is presented at Court she'll be able to make her dress for her.' The girls laughed uncertainly, as if they were not sure if that was meant for a joke or not, and his wife told him not to be 'a great donkey', but Laura felt uncomfortable. The only Court she had heard of was the County Court, to which a neighbour had recently been summoned, and the idea of being presented there was far from pleasant. . . .

Candleford seemed a very large and grand place to Laura, with its several streets meeting in a square where there were many large shop windows, with the blinds drawn because it was Sunday, and a doctor's house with a red lamp over the gate, and a church with a tall spire, and women and girls in light summer frocks and men in smart suits and white straw, boater-shaped hats.

But they were pulling up at a tall white house set back on a little green with a chestnut tree supporting scaffold poles and ladders and a sign which informed the public that James Dowland, Builder and Contractor, was ready and competent to undertake 'Constructions, Renovations, and Sanitary Work. Estimates Free'. . . .

The inside of the house seemed like a palace to Laura, after their own homely cottage. There were two parlours, one on each side of the front door, and in one of them a table was spread with decanters and wineglasses and dishes of cakes and fruit and biscuits. 'What a lovely dinner,' Laura whispered to her mother when they happened to be alone in the room for a moment.

'That's not dinner. It's refreshments,' she whispered back, and Laura thought 'refreshments' meant an extra nice dinner provided on such occasions. Then her father and Edmund came back from their hand-washing, Edmund bubbling over with some tale of a chain you could pull which brought water pouring down, 'More water than there is in the brook at home,' and their mother said, 'S-s-hush!' and added that she would explain later. Laura had not seen this marvel. She and her mother had taken off their hats and washed their hands in the best bedroom, a magnificent room with a four-poster bed with green curtains and a double washstand with a jug and basin each for them. 'You'll find the commode in that corner,' her auntie had said, and the commode turned out to be a kind of throne with carpeted steps and a lid which opened. But Laura was older than Edmund and knew it was rude to mention such things.

Uncle James Dowland now came in. He was a big man and an important-looking one, and seemed to fill even that large, well-proportioned room with his presence. At his approach Aunt Edith's stream of good-natured chatter ran dry, and Alma, who had been tiptoeing round the table, helping herself to a little from most of the dishes, sank down on the couch and pulled her short skirt over her knees. After she had been greeted by a heavy pat on the head, Laura shrank back behind her mother. Uncle James was so tall and stout and dark, with eye-brows so bushy and so thick a moustache, with so glossy a Sunday suit and so heavy a gold watchchain that, before him, the others present seemed to fade into the background. Except Laura's father, who nearly as tall as he was, though slighter, stood with him on the hearthrug, talking about their trade. It turned out afterwards to be the only safe subject. . . .

Their Aunt Edith was more attractive to children. She was pink and plump and had wavy grey hair and kind grey eyes. She was dressed in grey silk and when she stirred there was a faint scent of lavender. She looked kind and was kind; but, that discovered and acknowledged, there was little more to be said about her. Away from her husband and daughters she was talkative, running on from subject to subject, like a brook babbling. She greatly admired her husband, and every moment when alone with Laura's mother was devoted to his praise. It was James says this, and James did that, and stories to show how important and respected he was. In his presence she seemed a little afraid of him and she was certainly afraid of her daughters. It was 'What do you

think, dear?' or 'What would you do if you were me?' to the girls before she would express an opinion or make an arrangement. Then, to her sister-in-law, 'Of course, you see, Emmie, they've got different ideas to us, with all this education and getting to know people.' She had already informed her that they sometimes played tennis at the Rectory.

Laura thought the girls were conceited, and, although she could not have put it into words, felt they patronized her mother and her as poor relations; but perhaps she was wrong. It may only have been that they were so far removed in circumstances and interests that they had nothing in common. That was the only time Laura was to meet them upon anything like equal terms. They were away from home at the time of her next visit and grown-up before she saw them again. She was only just in time to catch the last flick of their skirts as they began to climb the social ladder which would take

them right out of her own life. . . .

It was all very rich and fine, but frightfully dull to a child who had come with such high expectations. They were back in the first parlour. The refreshments had disappeared and there was a green plush cloth on the table. Ethel and Alma had gone to Sunday School, where both took classes, and Laura had been given a book with views of Ramsgate to look at. The window blinds were drawn, for the sun was hot on the panes, and the room smelt of best clothes, furniture polish, and potpourri. Edmund was already asleep on his mother's knee and Laura was getting drowsy when the soft buzz of grown-up conversation which had been going on over her head was broken by sharp cries of 'Ireland', 'Home Rule', 'Gladstone says . . .' 'Lord Harrington says . . .' 'Joey Chamberlain says . . .' The two men had got on to the subject which her mother had dreaded.

'They're subjects of Queen Victoria, ain't they, same as we are,' his uncle insisted.

'Well, then, let 'em behave as such and be thankful to have a decent Government over 'em. Nice thing they'd make of governing themselves, and they no better than a lot of drunken savages.'

'How'd you like it if a foreign country invaded England . . .' her father began.

'I'd like to see 'em try it,' interposed her uncle.

'. . . invaded England and shed blood like water and burnt down your house and workshops and interfered with your religion. You'd want to get rid of 'em, I'll bet, and get back your independence.'

'Well, we did conquer 'em, didn't we? So let 'em learn who's their masters, I say, and if they won't toe the line, let our soldiers go over and make them.'

'How many Irishmen have you ever known personally?'

'If I'd only known one it'd be one too many; but, as a matter of fact, I've had several working for me at different times. Then there was Colonel Dimmock at Bradley, went bankrupt and let me in for more money than you're ever likely to earn.'

'Now, Bob!' pleaded Laura's mother.

'Now, James!' urged her aunt. 'You're not at a meeting now, but at home, and it's Sunday. What's Ireland to either of you. You've never been there and are never likely to, so have done with your arguing.'

Both men laughed a little and seemed ashamed of their vehemence, but her uncle could not forbear a parting shot.

'Tell you what,' he said, probably meaning it for a joke. 'In my opinion, the best way to settle the question would be to send over a shipload of whisky one day and a shipload of guns the next and they'd all get raving drunk and kill one another and save us the trouble.'

Robert stood up and his face was white with anger, but he only said a cold 'Good day' as he made for the door. His wife and sister ran to him and seized an arm each and his brother-in-law told him not to be a fool. 'It's only politics,' he said. 'You take things too seriously. Come, sit down, and Edith'll tell the girl to bring in a cup of tea before you go on to Ann's.' But Robert walked out of the house and away down the street after saying over his shoulder to his wife, 'See you later.'

He had no sense of humour. None of them had at

159

that moment. Laura's mother was all apologies. Her uncle, still angry, but a little ashamed, said he was sorry *for her*. Her aunt wiped her eyes on a pretty lace-edged handkerchief and Laura's needed wiping, for was not their long-looked-for day ruined if their lovely drive behind Polly had only led to this.

It was her mother, who did not pretend to be well-bred, yet always managed to do or say the right thing, who eased the situation by saying: 'Well, he'll have to come back presently to harness the horses and he'll be sorry enough by that time, I dare say, and I think I *will* have that cup of tea, if Bertha's got the kettle boiling. Just a cup to drink. Nothing more to eat, really. Then we must be getting on.'

After a decent interval, during which everybody tried to talk as though nothing had happened, the two children with their mother set out to follow their father to Aunt Ann's, Laura dragging behind a little, for the sun was hot and she was tired and not sure that she liked Candleford.

She soon cheered up; there was so much to see. Houses, houses all the way, not rows of houses, all alike, like peas in a pod, but big and little, tall and low, with old grey walls between with broken bottle-glass on the coping and fruit trees waving in gardens behind, and queer door-knockers and little shed-like porches, and people walking in their thin best shoes on the cobblestones with bunches of flowers, or prayerbooks, or beer jugs in their hands.

Once, at a turning, they caught a glimpse of a narrow lane of poor houses with ragged washing slung on lines between windows and children sitting on doorsteps. 'Is that a slum, Mother?' asked Laura, for she recognized some of the features described in the Sunday-school stories.

'Of course not,' said her mother crossly; then, after they had passed the turning: 'Don't speak so loud. Somebody might hear you and not like it. Folks who live in slums don't call them that. They're used to it and it seems all right to them. And why should you worry about things like that. You'd do better to mind your own business.'

Her own business! Wasn't it her business to be sorry for people who lived in slums and had no food or bed and a drunken father, or a landlord ready to turn them out in the snow. Hadn't her mother herself nearly cried when she read *Froggy's Little Brother* aloud to them? Laura could have cried then, in the middle of Candleford, at the thought of the time when Froggy took home the bloater as a treat and his poor little brother was too ill to eat any.

But they had come to a place where they could see green fields and a winding river with willows beside it. Facing them with its back to the fields was a row of shops, the last in the town on that side, and in the window of the shop they were approaching was nothing but one lady's top boot, beautifully polished and standing on an amber velvet cushion with an amber velvet curtain behind it. Above the window was a notice, unreadable to Laura then, but read by her many times afterwards, which said: 'Ladies' boots and shoes made to order. Best Materials. Perfect Workmanship. Fit Guaranteed. Ladies' Hunting Boots a Speciality.'

Their Uncle Tom had what was at that time called 'a snug little business'. It was a common thing then for people of all classes, excepting the very poorest, to have their footwear made to measure. In a large workshop across the yard at the back of the house and shop, workmen and apprentices scraped and hammered and sewed all day, making and mending. Uncle Tom's own workshop was a back room of the house, with a door opening out on to the yard, across which he came and went dozens of times a day to and from the main workshop. He made the hunting boots there and sewed the uppers of the more delicate makes, and there he fitted the customers, excepting the hunting ladies, who tried their boots on in the best parlour, Uncle Tom kneeling on the carpet before them like a courtier before a queen.

But all this Laura found out afterwards. On that first visit the front door flew open before they had reached it and they were surrounded by cousins and kissed and hugged and led to where Aunt Ann stood in the doorway.

Laura had never known any one like her Aunt Ann. The neighbours at home were kind in their rough way, but they were so bent on doing their best for themselves and those belonging to them that, excepting in times of illness or trouble, they had little feeling to spare for others. Her mother was kind and sensible and loved her children dearly, but she did not believe in showing too much tenderness towards them or in 'giving herself away' to the world at large. Aunt Ann gave herself away with every breath she drew. No one who heard her gentle voice or looked into her fine dark eyes could doubt her loving nature. Her husband laughed at what he called her 'softness' and said that customers calling in a great rage to complain that their shoes had not been delivered to time had stayed to tell the full story of their lives. For her own children she had sweet, pet names, and Edmund was soon her 'little lover' and Laura her 'Pussikins'. Except for her eyes and the dark, satiny hair which rippled in waves flat to her head, she was a plain-looking woman, pale and thin of face and of figure so flat that, with her hair parted in the middle and in the long, straight frocks she wore, she reminded Laura of Mrs Noah in the toy ark she had given Edmund at Christmas. That impression, a bony embrace, and a soft, warm kiss were all Laura had time for before she was borne on a stream of cousins straight through the house to an arbour in the garden where her father and uncle sat with a jug and glasses on a table between them

and their pipes in their mouths. They were talking amiably together, although, only that morning, her father had spoken of her uncle as 'a snob' and her mother had protested, 'But he's not a common cobbler, Bob. He's a master man, and he makes more than he mends.'

If Laura's Uncle Tom was a snob by trade, there was nothing else snobbish about him, for he was one of the most liberal-minded men she was ever to know and one of the wisest. He was a Liberal in politics, too, and no doubt that accounted for her father's air of friendliness and ease. They were settling the Irish question, for the old familiar catchwords caught her ear, and it was rather an absent-minded uncle who stroked her hair and told the girls to take her to play in the orchard, but not to let the little boy go tumbling in the river, or their mother would have all those cakes she had been making left on her hands. . . .

Gradually, she became able to distinguish between the new faces and to discover the name for each. There was Molly, the eldest, a motherly little person with a plump, soft figure, red-gold hair, and freckles on the bridge of her nose. Annie had reddish hair, too, but was smaller than Molly and had no freckles. Nelly was dark, quick in her movements, and said things that made people laugh. 'Sharp as a needle,' said Laura's father afterwards. Amy, the youngest girl, was Laura's own age. She had a red bow on her dark curls, but Laura did not need to look at the bow, except to admire it, because Amy was smaller than the others.

Johnny was the youngest of all, but by far the most important, for he was a boy, and a boy who came at the end of a long string of girls. Johnny must have anything he wanted, no matter to whom it belonged. If Johnny fell down, he must be picked up and comforted, and around Johnny, when he approached the river, red heads and dark heads drew to form a bodyguard. Rather a baby, thought Laura, although the same age as Edmund, who needed no attention at all, but went and stood on the bank and threw down twigs to float and called them ships; then ran, throwing up his heels like a young colt and lay on his back in the grass with his legs sticking up. . . .

The children had plenty to discuss. 'Can you read?' 'When are you going to school?' 'What's Lark Rise like?' 'Only a few houses – all fields?' 'Where do you buy things if there are no shops?' 'Do you like Molly's hair? Most people hate red and they call her "ginger" at school; but Mr Collier, that's our Vicar, says it's lovely, and a customer told Mother that if she liked to have it cut off she could sell it for pounds and pounds. Some ladies would pay anything to have it to put on their own heads. Yes, didn't you know that some people wear false hair? Aunt Edith has a switch? I've seen it, hanging on her dressing-table in the morning; that's what makes her hair bunch out so at the back.' 'And your hair's nice, too, Laura,' said Molly generously, picking out Laura's best feature. 'I like the way it runs like water all down your back.'

'My mother can sit on her hair when it's down,' boasted Laura, and the cousins were impressed, for a great deal was thought of quantity in those days, of hair as of other things.

All the girls were going to school in the town as yet, but soon Molly and Nellie were to go to Miss Bussell's for a year each to be 'finished'. When, later, Laura asked her father if Johnny would go to Miss Bussell's, too, he laughed and said, 'Of course not. It's a girls' school. For the daughters of gentlemen, says the brass plate on the door, and that means for the daughters of a chimney sweep, if he can afford to pay.'

'Then where will Johnny go?' she persisted, and her father said, 'Eton, I s'pose,' which rather alarmed Laura because she thought he had said 'eaten'. She was relieved when he added, 'But I doubt if that'll be good enough. They'll have to build a special school on purpose for Johnny.'

What surprised Laura most as she listened to her cousins that afternoon was that they spoke of school as if they liked it. The hamlet children hated school. It was prison to them, and from the very beginning they counted the years until they would be able to leave. But Molly and Nellie and Amy said school was great fun. Annie did not like it so much.

'A-h-h! Who's bottom of her class!' laughed Nell.

But Molly said, 'Never mind her, Annie. She may be good at lessons, but she can't sew for nuts, and you're going to get the needlework prize with that baby's frock you're making. Ask her what Miss Pridham said when she examined her herring-boning.'

Then a voice from the upper garden called them in to tea. Just the kind of tea Laura liked, bread and butter and jam and a cake and some little cakes, a little more of everything than they had at home, but not the rich, bewildering abundance of the 'refreshments'.

She liked her cousins' house, too. It was old, with little flights of steps going up or down in unexpected places. Aunt Ann's parlour had a piano across one corner and a soft green carpet the colour of faded moss. The windows were wide open and there was a delicious scent of wallflowers and tea and cake and cobbler's wax. They had tea out of the silver teapot at the large round table in the parlour that day. Afterwards, they always had tea in the kitchen, much the nicest room in the house, with its two windows with window seats and brass warming pans and candlesticks and strips of red-and-blue striped matting on the stone floor.

That day, because they were having tea in the parlour, there was not room at the table for all, and Edmund and Johnny were seated at a side table with their backs to the wall, so that their respective mothers could keep an eye on them. But there was still so much talking going on among the elders that the little boys were forgotten until Johnny asked for more cake. When his mother handed him a slice he said it was too large, and, when halved, too small, and, finally, left the portion he had accepted in crumbs upon his plate, which shocked Edmund and Laura, who, at home, had to eat whatever was put upon their plates, and 'no leavings allowed'.

'Spoilt to death, regularly spoilt' was their mother's verdict when Johnny was spoken of afterwards, and perhaps at that time he was spoilt. He could scarcely escape spoiling, being the only and long-desired boy, coming after so many girls and then turning out to be the only delicate one of the family. He was young for his age and slow in developing; but there was fine stuff in Johnny. As a young man he was deeply religious, a non-smoker, a non-drinker and a non-card-player, and served the altar set up on many a battlefield during the 1914-18 War, and all this needed character in the atmosphere of Army life.

---IX---

CANDLEFORD GREEN

ON one of her visits to Candleford, Laura herself found a friend, and one whose influence was to shape the whole outward course of her life.

An old friend of her mother's named Dorcas Lane kept the Post Office at Candleford Green, and one year, when she heard that Laura was staying so near her, she asked her and her cousins to go over to tea. Only Molly would go; the others said it was too hot for walking, that Miss Lane was faddy and old-fashioned, and that there was no one to talk to at Candleford Green and nothing to see. So Laura, Edmund, and Molly went.

Candleford Green was at that time a separate village. In a few years it was to become part of Candleford. Already the rows of villas were stretching out towards it; but as yet the green with its spreading oak with the white-painted seats, its roofed-in well with the chained bucket, its church spire soaring out of trees, and its clusters of old cottages, was untouched by change.

Miss Lane's house was a long, low white one, with the Post Office at one end and a blacksmith's forge at the other. On the turf of the green in front of the door was a circular iron platform with a hole in the middle which was used for putting on tyres to wagon and cart wheels, for she was wheelwright as well as blacksmith and postmistress. She did not work in the forge herself; she dressed in silks of which the colours were brighter than those usually worn then by women of her age and had tiny white hands which she seldom soiled. Hers was the brain of the business.

To go to see Cousin Dorcas, as they had been told to call her, was an exciting event to Laura and Edmund, for they hoped to be shown her famous telegraph machine. There had been some talk about it at home when their parents heard it had been installed, and their mother, who had seen one, described it as a sort of clock face, but with letters instead of figures, 'and when you turn the handle,' she said, 'the hand goes round and you can spell out words on it, and that sends the hand round on the clock face at the other Post Office where it's for, and they just write it down, pop it into an envelope, and send it where it's addressed.'

'And then they know somebody's going to die,' put in Edmund.

'After they've paid three and sixpence,' said their father, rather bitterly, for an agitation was being worked up in the hamlet against having to pay that crushing sum for the delivery of a telegram. 'For Hire of Man and Horse, 3s. 6d.' was written upon the envelope and that sum had to be found and paid before the man on the horse would part with the telegram. But about that time, the innkeeper, tired of having to lend three and sixpence with little prospect of getting it back, every time the news arrived that some neighbour's father or mother or sister or aunt was 'sinking fast' or had 'passed peacefully away this morning', had, in collaboration with a few neighbours of whom the children's father was one, written a formal and much-thought-out protest to the Postmaster General, which resulted in men coming with long chains to measure the whole length of the road between the hamlet and the Post Office in the market town. The distance was found to be a few feet under, instead of over, the three-miles limit of the free delivery of telegrams. This made quite an interesting little story for Laura to tell Cousin Dorcas. 'And to think of those poor things having paid that sum! As much as a man could earn in a day and a half's hard work,' was her comment, and there was something in the way she said it that made Laura feel that, although, as her cousins said, Miss Lane might be peculiar, it was a nice kind of peculiarity.

Laura liked her looks, too. She was then about fifty, a little, birdlike woman in her kingfisher silk dress, with snapping black eyes, a longish nose, and black hair plaited into a crown on the top of her head. . . .

She showed Laura her house, from attic to cellar, and what a house it was! Her parents had lived in it, and her grandparents, and it was her delight to keep all the old family possessions just as she had inherited them. Other people might scrap their solid old furniture and replace it with plush-covered suites and what-nots and painted milking-stools and Japanese fans; but Dorcas had the taste to prefer good old oak and mahogany and brass, and the strength of mind to dare to be thought old-fashioned. So the grandfather's clock in the front kitchen still struck the hours as it had done on the day of the Battle of Waterloo. The huge, heavy oak table at the head of which she carved for the workmen and maid, sitting in higher or lower seats according to degree, was older still. There was a legend that it had been made in the kitchen by the then village carpenter and was too large to remove without taking it to pieces. The bedrooms still had their original four-posters, one of them with blue-and-white check curtains, the yarn of which had been spun by her grandmother on the spinning wheel lately rescued from the attic, repaired and placed with the telegraph instrument in the parlour. On the dresser shelves were pewter plates and dishes, with a few pieces of old willow-pattern 'to liven them up', as she said; and in the chimney corner, where Laura

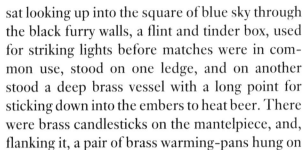

sat looking up into the square of blue sky through the black furry walls, a flint and tinder box, used for striking lights before matches were in common use, stood on one ledge, and on another stood a deep brass vessel with a long point for sticking down into the embers to heat beer. There were brass candlesticks on the mantelpiece, and, flanking it, a pair of brass warming-pans hung on the wall. These were no longer in use, nor was the sandbox for drying wet ink instead of using blotting-paper, nor the nest of wooden chopping bowls, nor the big brewing copper in the back kitchen, but they were piously preserved in their old places, and, with them, as many of the old customs as could be made to fit in with modern requirements.

The grandfather's clock was kept exactly half an hour fast, as it had always been, and, by its time, the household rose at six, breakfasted at seven and dined at noon; while mails were despatched and telegrams timed by the new Post Office clock, which showed correct Greenwich time, received by wire at ten o'clock every morning.

Miss Lane's mind kept time with both clocks. Although she loved the past and tried to preserve its spirit as well as its relics, in other ways she was in advance of her own day. She read a good deal, not poetry, or pure literature – she had not the right kind of mind for that – but she took in *The Times* and kept herself well-informed of what was going on in the world, especially in the way of invention and scientific discovery. Probably she was the only person on or around the Green who had heard the name of Darwin. Others of her interests were international relationships and what is now called big business. She had shares in railways and the local Canal Company, which was daring for a woman in her position, and there was an affair called the Iceland Moss Litter Company for news of which watch had to be kept when, later, Laura was reading the newspaper aloud to her. . . .

She had arranged her Post Office with its shining counter, brass scales, and stamps, postal orders, and multiplicity of official forms neatly pigeonholed, in what had been a broad passage which ran through the house from the front door to the garden. The door which led from this into the front kitchen, where meals were taken, marked the boundary between the new world and the old. In after days, when Laura had read a little history, it gave her endless pleasure to notice the sudden transition from one world to the other.

It was still the custom in that trade for unmarried workmen to live-in with the families of their employers; and, at mealtimes, when the indoor contingent was already seated, sounds of pumping and sluicing water over hands and faces would come from the paved courtyard outside. Then 'the men', as they were always called, would appear, rolling their leather aprons up around their waists as they tiptoed to their places at table. . . .

There, the journeymen's place was definitely below the salt. At the head of the long, solid oak table sat 'the mistress' with an immense dish of meat before her, carving knife in hand. Then came a reserved space, sometimes occupied by visitors, but more often blank table-cloth; then Matthew's chair, and, after that, another, smaller blank space, just sufficient to mark the difference in degree between a foreman and ordinary workmen. Beyond that, the three young men sat in a row at the end of the table, facing the mistress. Zillah, the maid, had a little round table to herself by the wall. Unless important visitors were present, she joined freely in the conversation; but the three young men seldom opened their mouths excepting to shovel in food. . . .

As a child, Laura thought the young men were poorly treated and was inclined to pity them; but, afterwards, she found they were under an age-old discipline, supposed, in some mysterious way, to fit them for becoming in their turn master-men. Under this system, such and such an article of food was not suitable for the men; the men must have something substantial – boiled beef and dumplings, or a thick cut off a gammon, or a joint of beef. When they came in to go to bed on a cold night, they could be offered hot spiced beer, but not elderberry wine. They must not be encouraged to talk and you must never discuss family affairs in their presence, or they might become familiar; in short, they must be kept in their place, because they were 'the men'.

Until that time, or a few years earlier in more advanced districts, these distinctions had suited the men as well as they had done the employers. Their huge meals and their beds in a row in the large attic were part of their wages, and as long as it was excellent food and the beds were good feather beds with plenty of blankets, they had all they expected or wished for indoors. More would have embarrassed them. They had their own lives outside. . . .

All kinds of horses came to the forge to be shod: heavy cart-horses, standing quiet and patient; the baker's and grocer's and butcher's van horses; poor old screws belonging to gipsies or fish-hawkers; and an occasional hunter, either belonging to some visitor to the neighbourhood or one from a local stable which had cast a shoe and could not wait until the regular visiting day. There were a few donkeys in the neighbourhood, and they, too, had to be shod; but always by the youngest shoeing smith, for it would have been beneath the dignity of his seniors to become the butt for the wit of the passers-by. 'He-haw! He-haw!' they would shout. 'Somebody tell me now, which is top-most, man or beast, for danged if I can see any difference betwixt 'em?'

Most of the horses were very patient; but a few would plunge and kick and rear when approached. These Matthew himself shod and, under his skilful handling, they would quiet down immediately. He had only to put his hand on the mane and whisper a few words in the ear. It was probably the hand and voice which soothed them; but it was generally believed that he whispered some charm which had power over them, and he rather encouraged this idea by saying when questioned: 'I only speaks to 'em in their own language.'. . .

Secure in the knowledge of their own importance in the existing scheme of things, the blacksmiths boasted: 'Come what may, a good smith'll never want for a job, for whatever may come of this new cast-iron muck in other ways, the horses'll always have to be shod, and they can't do that in a foundry!'

Yet, as iron will bend to different uses, so will the workers in iron. Twenty years later the younger of that generation of smiths were painting above their shop doors, 'Motor Repairs a Speciality', and, greatly daring, taking mechanism to pieces which they had no idea how they were going to put together again. They made many mistakes, which passed undetected because the owners had no more knowledge than they had of the inside of 'the dratted thing', and they soon learned by experiment sufficient to enable them to put on a wise air of authority. Then the legend over the door was repainted, 'Motor Expert', and expert many of them became in a surprisingly short time, for they brought the endless patience and ingenuity of the craftsman to the new mechanism, plus his adaptable skill. . . .

EXIT LAURA

HER mother was stooping to take something out of the oven and as she looked down upon her, Laura noticed for the first time that her looks were changing. The blue eyes were bluer than ever, but the pink and white of her face was weathering. Her figure was hardening, too; slim young grace was turning to thin wiriness; and a few grey threads showed in her hair at the temples. Her mother was growing old, soon she would die, thought Laura with sudden compunction, and then how sorry she would be for giving her so much trouble.

But her mother, still on the right side of forty, did not think of herself as ageing and had no thought of dying for a good many more years to come. As it turned out, barely half of her life was over.

'Gracious, how you are shooting up!' she said cheerfully, as she rose and stretched herself. 'I shall soon have to stand tiptoe to tie your hair-ribbon. Have a potato cake? I found young Biddy had laid an egg this morning, her first and not very big, so I thought I'd make us a cake for tea of those cold potatoes in the pantry. A bit of sugar can always be spared. That's cheap enough.'

Laura ate the cake with great relish, for it was delicious, straight from the oven, and it was also a mark of her mother's favour; the little ones were not allowed to eat between meals.

Her father had put up a swing for the younger children in the wash-house. She could hear one of them now, crying, 'Higher! Higher!' Except for the baby, asleep in the cradle, her mother and she were alone in the room, which, on that dull day, was aglow with firelight. Her mother's pastry board and rolling-pin still stood on a white cloth on one end of the table, and the stew for dinner, mostly composed of vegetables, but very savoury-smelling, simmered upon the hob. She had a sudden impulse to tell her mother how much she loved her; but in the early 'teens such feelings cannot be put into words, and all she could do was to praise the potato cake.

But perhaps her look conveyed something of what she felt, for, that evening, her mother, after speaking of her own father, who had been dead three or four years, added: 'You are the only one I can talk to about him. Your father and he never got on together and the others were too young when he died to remember him. Lots of things happened before they were born that you'll always remember, so I shall always have somebody to talk to about the old times.'

From that day a new relationship was established and grew between them. Her mother was not kinder to Laura than she had been, for she had always been kindness itself, but she took her more into her confidence, and Laura was happy again.

But, as so often happens when two human beings have come to understand each other, they were soon to be parted. In the early spring a letter came from Candleford saying that Dorcas Lane wanted a learner for her Post Office work and thought Laura

would do, if her parents were willing. Although she was not one for much gadding about, she said, it was irksome to be always tied to the house during Post Office hours. 'Not that I expect her to stay with me for ever,' she added. 'She'll want to do better for herself later on, and, when that time comes I'll speak to Head Office and we shall see what we shall see.'

So, one morning in May, Polly and the spring-cart drew up at the gate and Laura's little trunk, all new and shiny black with her initials in brass-headed nails, was hoisted into the back seat, and Laura in a new frock – grey cashmere with a white lace collar and the new leg-of-mutton sleeves – climbed up beside her father, who was taking a day off to drive Polly.

'Good-bye, Laura. Good-bye. Good-bye. Don't forget to write to me.'

'And to me, and address it to my very own self,' cried the little sisters.

'You be a good gal an' do what you're told an' you'll get on like a house afire,' called a

kindly neighbour from her doorway.

'Wrap every penny stamp up in a smile,' advised the inn-keeper, closing his double gates after Polly's exit.

As Polly trotted on, Laura turned to look across fields green with spring wheat to the huddle of grey cottages where she knew her mother was thinking about her, and tears came into her eyes.

Her father looked at her in surprise, then said kindly but grudgingly: 'Well, 'tis your home, such as it is, I suppose.'

Yes, with all its limitations, the hamlet was home to her. There she had spent her most impressionable years and, although she was never to live there again for more than a few weeks at a time, she would bear their imprint through life.

CANDLEFORD GREEN

—— XI ——

FROM ONE SMALL WORLD TO ANOTHER

LAURA sat up beside her father on the high front seat of the spring-cart and waved to the neighbours. 'Good-bye, Laura! Good-bye!' they called. 'Mind you be a good gal, now!' and Laura, as she turned to smile and wave back to them, tried not to look too conscious of her new frock and hat and the brand-new trunk (with her initials) roped on to the back seat.

As the cart moved on, more women came to their doors to see what the sound of wheels meant at that time in the morning. It was not the coalman's or the fish-hawker's day, the baker was not due for hours, and the appearance of any other wheeled vehicle than theirs always caused a mild sensation in that secluded hamlet. When they saw Laura and her new trunk, the women remained on their doorsteps to wave their farewells, then, before the cart had turned into the road from the rutted lane, little groups began forming.

Her going seemed to be causing quite a stir in the hamlet. Not because the sight of a young girl going out in the world to earn her own living was an uncommon one there – all the hamlet girls left home for that purpose, some of them at a much earlier age than Laura – but they usually went on foot, carrying bundles, or their fathers pushed their boxes on wheelbarrows to the railway station in the nearest town the night before, while, for Laura's departure, the innkeeper's pony and cart had been hired.

That, of course, was because Candleford Green, although only eight miles distant, was on another line of railway than that which ran through the market town, and to have gone there by train would have meant two changes and a long wait at the Junction; but the spring-cart brought a spice of novelty into her departure which made 'something to talk about', as the saying went there. At the beginning of the eighteen-nineties any new subject for conversation was precious in such places.

Laura was fourteen and a half, and the thick pigtail of hair which had so far hung down her back had that morning been looped up once and tied with a big black ribbon bow on her neck. When they had first known that she was to go to work in the Post Office at Candleford Green her mother had wondered if she ought not to wear her hair done up with hairpins, grown-up fashion, but when she saw a girl behind the Post Office counter at Sherston wearing hers in a loop with a bow she had felt sure that that was the proper way for Laura to do hers. So the ribbon was bought – black, of course, for her mother said the bright-coloured ribbons most country girls wore made them look like horses, all plaited and beribboned for a fair. 'And mind you sponge and press it often,' she had said, 'for it cost good money. And when you come to buy your own clothes, always buy the best you can afford. It pays in the end.' But Laura could not bear to think of her mother just then; the parting was too recent. . . .

In the early 'nineties the change which had for some time been going on in the outer world had reached Candleford Green. A few old-fashioned country homes, such as that of Miss Lane, might still be seen there, especially among those of the farming class, and long-established family businesses still existed, side by side with those newly established or brought up to date; but, as the older house-holders died and the proprietors of the old-fashioned businesses died or retired, the old gave place to the new.

Tastes and ideas were changing. Quality was less in demand than it had been. The old solid, hand-made productions, into which good materials and many hours of patient skilled craftsmanship had been put, were comparatively costly. The new machine-made goods cost less and had the further attraction of a meretricious smartness. Also they were fashionable, and most people preferred them on that account.

'Time, like an ever-rolling stream, bears all its sons away,' and its daughters, too, and the tastes and ideas of each generation, together with its ideals and conventions, go rolling downstream with it like so much debris. But, because the generations overlap, the change is gradual. In the country at the time now recorded, the day of the old skilled master-craftsman, though waning, was not over.

Across the green, almost opposite to the post office, stood a substantial cottage, end to end with a carpenters' shop. In most weathers the big double door of the workshop stood open and white-aproned workmen with their feet ankle-deep in shavings could be seen sawing and planing and shaping at the benches, with, behind them, a window framing a glimpse of a garden with old-fashioned flowers and a grape-vine draping a grey wall.

There lived and worked the three Williams, father, son, and grandson. With the help of a couple of journeymen, they not only did all the carpentry and joinery of the district at a time when no doors or mantelpieces or window-frames came ready made from abroad, but they also made and mended furniture for the use of the living and made coffins for the dead. There was no rival shop. The elder William was the carpenter of the village, just as Miss Lane was the postmistress and Mr Coulsdon the vicar.

Although less popular than the smithy as a gathering place, the carpenters' shop had also its habitués: older and graver men, as a rule, especially choirmen, for the eldest William played the organ in church and the middle William was choirmaster. Old Mr Stokes not only played the organ, but he had built it with his own hands, and these services to the Church and to music had given him a unique local standing. But he was almost as much valued for his great experience and his known wisdom. To him the villagers went in trouble or difficulty, and he was never known to fail them. He had been Miss Lane's father's close and intimate friend and was then her own.

At the time Laura knew him he was nearly eighty and much troubled by asthma, but he still worked at his trade occasionally, with his long, lean form swathed in a white apron and his full white beard buttoned into his waistcoat; and, on summer evenings, when the rolling peal of the organ came from the open door of the church, passers-by would say: 'That's old Mr Stokes playing, I'll lay! And he's playing his own music, too, I shouldn't wonder.' Sometimes he *was* playing his own music, for he would improvise for hours, but he loved more to play for his own pleasure the music of the masters.

The second William was unlike his father in appearance, being short and thick of figure while his father was as straight and almost as thin as a lath. His face resembled that of Dante Gabriel Rossetti so closely that Laura, on seeing the portrait of that poet-painter in later years, exclaimed, 'Mr William!' For, of course, he was called 'Mr William'. His father was always spoken of respectfully as 'Mr Stokes', and his nephew as 'Young Willie.'

Like his father, Mr William was both musician and craftsman of the old school, and it was naturally expected that as a matter of course these gifts would descend to the third William. It had been a proud day for old Mr Stokes when young Willie's indentures were signed, for he thought he saw in them an assured future for the old family business. When he was at rest, and his son, there would still be a William Stokes, Carpenter and Joiner, of Candleford Green, and, after that, perhaps, still another William to follow.

But Willie himself was not so sure. He had been legally apprenticed to his grandfather's business, as was the custom in family establishments in those days, rather because it was the line laid down for him than because he desired to become a carpenter. His work in the shop was to him but work, not a fine art or a religion, and for the music so sacred to his elders he had but a moderate taste.

He was a tall, slim boy of sixteen, with beautiful hazel eyes and a fair – too fair – pink-and-white complexion. Had his mother or his grandmother been alive, his alternating fits of lassitude and devil-may-care high spirits would have been recognized as a sign that he was outgrowing his strength and that his health needed care. But the only woman in his grandfather's house was a middle-aged cousin of the middle William, who acted as housekeeper: a hard, gaunt, sour-looking woman whose thoughts and energies were centred upon keeping the house spotless. When the front door of their house was opened upon the small bare hall, with its grandfather's clock and oil-cloth floor-covering patterned with lilies, an intruding nose was met by the clean, cold smell of soap and furniture polish. Everything in that house which could be scrubbed was scrubbed to a snowy whiteness; not a chair or a rug or a picture-frame was ever a hairbreadth out of place; horsehair chair and sofa coverings were polished to a cold slipperiness, table-tops might have served as mirrors, and an air of comfortless order pervaded the whole place. It was indeed a model house in the matter of cleanliness, but as a home for a delicate, warm-hearted orphan boy it fell short.

The kitchen was the only inhabited room. There the three generations of Williams took their meals, and there they carefully removed their shoes before retiring to the bedrooms which were sleeping-places only. To come home with wet clothes on a rainy day was accounted a crime. The drying of them 'messed up the place', so Willie, who was the only one of the three to be out in such weather, would change surreptitiously and leave his clothes to dry as they might, or not dry. His frequent colds left him with a cough that lingered every year into the spring. 'A churchyard cough,' the older villagers said, and shook their heads knowingly. But his grandfather did not appear to notice this. Although he loved him tenderly, he had too many other interests to be able to keep a close watch over his grandson's physical well-being. He left that to the cousin, who was absorbed in her housework and already felt it a hardship to have what she called 'a great hulking hobble-de-hoy' in the house to mess up her floors and rugs and made enough cooking and washing up for a regiment.

Willie did not care for the music his grandfather and uncle loved. He preferred the banjo and such popular songs as 'Oh, dem Golden Slippers' and 'Two Lovely Black Eyes' to organ fugues – except in church, where he sometimes sang the anthem, looking like an angel in his white surplice.

181

Yet, in other ways, he had a great love of and craving for beauty. 'I do like deep, rich colours – violet and crimson and the blue of these delphiniums – don't you?' he said to Laura in Miss Lane's garden one day. Laura loved those colours, too. She was almost ashamed to answer the questions in the Confession Books of her more fashionable friends: *Favourite colours?* Purple and crimson. *Favourite flowers?* The red rose. *Favourite poet?* Shakespeare. The answers made her appear so unoriginal. She almost envied previous writers in the books their preferences when she read: *Favourite flower?* Petunia, orchid, or sweet-pea; but she had not as yet the social wit to say, 'Favourite flower? After the rose, of course?' or to pay mere lip service to Shakespeare, so she was obliged to appear obvious.

Willie was fond of reading, too and did not object to poetry. Somehow he had got possession of an old shattered copy of an anthology called *A Thousand and One Gems* and when he came to tea with Miss Lane, who had known his mother and had a special affection for him, he would bring this book, and after office hours Laura and he would sit among the nut-trees at the bottom of the garden and take turns at reading aloud from it. . . .

But one incident she shared with Willie remained more vivid in her memory than the poetry readings or the scrapes he got into with other boys, such as being let down into a well by the chain to rescue a duck which had spent a day and a night, quacking loudly, as it searched in vain for a shore to that deep, narrow pool into which it had tumbled, or the time when the hayrick was on fire and, against the advice of older men, he climbed to the top to beat the burning thatch with a rake.

She had gone one day to his home with a message from Miss Lane to the housekeeper and, finding no one at home in the house, had crossed the yard to a shed where Willie was working. He was sorting out planks and, intending to tease and perhaps to shock her, he showed her a pile at the farther end of the shed in the semi-darkness. 'Just look at these,' he said. 'Here! Come right in and put your hand on them. Know what they're for? Well, I'll tell you. They're all and every one of them sides for coffins. I wonder who this one's for, and this and this. This nice little narrow one may be for you; it looks about the right size. And this one at the bottom' – touching it with his toes – 'may be for that very chap we can hear kicking up such a row with his whistling outside. They're all booked for somebody, mostly somebody we know, but there aren't any names written on them.'

Laura pretended to laugh and called him a horrid boy, but the bright day seemed to her suddenly to become dark and cold, and, afterwards, whenever she passed that shed she shivered and thought of the pile of coffin boards waiting in the half-darkness until they should be needed to make coffins for people now going happily about the green on their business and passing the shed without a shudder. The elm or the oak which had

yet to make her coffin must then have been growing green, somewhere or other, and Willie had no coffin tree growing for him, for his was a soldier's grave out on the veld in South Africa.

He, the youngest, was the first of the three Williams to go. Soon after, the middle William died suddenly while working at his bench, and his father followed him next winter. Then the carpenters' shop was demolished to make way for a builder's showroom with baths and tiled fireplaces and w.c. pans in the window, and only the organ in church and pieces of good woodwork in houses remained to remind those who had known them of the three Williams.

Squeezed back to leave space for a small front garden, between the Stores and the carpenters' shop, was a tall, narrow cottage with three sash windows, one above the other, which almost filled the front wall. In the lowest window stood a few bottles of bullseyes and other boiled sweets, and above them hung a card which said: *Dressmaking and Plain Sewing.* This was the home of one of the two postwomen who, every morning, carried the letters to outlying houses off the regular postman's beat.

Unlike her colleague, who was old, grumpy and snuffy, Mrs Macey was no ordinary countrywoman. She spoke well and had delicate, refined, if somewhat worn, features, with nice grey eyes and a figure of the kind of which country people said: 'So-and-So'd manage to look well-dressed if she went round wrapped in a dishcloth.' And Mrs Macey did manage to look well-dressed, although her clothes were usually shabby and sometimes peculiar. For most of the year on her round she wore a long grey cloth coat of the kind then known as an 'ulster', and, for headgear, a man's black bowler hat

draped with a black lace veil with short ends hanging at the back. This hat, Miss Lane said, was a survival of a fashion of ten years before. Laura had never seen another like it, but worn as Mrs Macey wore it, over a head of softly waving dark hair drawn down into a little tight knob on the neck, it was decidedly becoming. Instead of plodding or sauntering country fashion, Mrs Macey walked firmly and quickly, as if with a destination in view.

Excepting Miss Lane, who was more of a patron than a friend, Mrs Macey had no friends in the village. She had been born and had lived as a

184

child on a farm near Candleford Green where her father was then bailiff; but before she had grown up her family had gone away and all that was known locally of fifteen years of her life was that she had married and lived in London. Then, four or five years before Laura knew her, she had returned to the village with her only child, at that time a boy of seven, and taken the cottage next to the Stores and put the card in the window. When the opportunity offered, Miss Lane obtained for her the letter-carrier's post and, with the four shillings a week pay for that, a weekly postal order for the same amount from some mysterious organization (the Freemasons, it was whispered, but that was a mere guess) and the money earned by her sewing, she was able in those days and in that locality to live and bring up her boy in some degree of comfort.

She was not a widow, but she never mentioned her husband unless questioned, when she would say something about 'travelling abroad with his gentleman', leaving her hearer to conclude that he was a valet or something of that kind. Some people said she had no husband and never had had one, she had only invented one as a blind to account for her child, but Miss Lane nipped such suspicions in the bud by saying authoritatively that she had good reasons which she was not at liberty to reveal for saying that Mrs Macey had a husband still living.

Laura liked Mrs Macey and often crossed the green to her house in the evening to buy a screw of sweets or to try on a garment which was being made or turned or lengthened for her. It was as cosy a little place as can be imagined. The ground floor of the house had formerly been one largish room with a stone floor, but, by erecting a screen to enclose the window and fireplace and cut off the draughty outer portion, where water vessels and cooking utensils were kept, Mrs Macey had contrived a tiny inner living-room. In this she had a table for meals, a sofa and easy chair, and her sewing-machine. There were rugs on the floor and pictures on the walls and plenty of cushions about. These were all of good quality – relics, no doubt, of the much larger home she had had during her married life. . . .

Her Tommy was a quiet, thoughtful little lad with the man-of-the-house air of responsibility sometimes worn by fatherless only sons. He liked to wind up the clock, let out the cat, and lock the house door at night. Once when he had brought home a blouse which Mrs Macey had been making out of an old muslin frock for Laura and with it the bill, for some now incredibly small amount – a shilling at the most, probably ninepence – Laura, by way of a mild joke, handed him her pencil and said, 'Perhaps you'll give me a receipt for the money?' 'With pleasure,' he said in his best grown-up manner. 'But it's really not necessary. We shan't charge you for it again.' Laura smiled at that 'we', denoting a partnership in which the junior partner was so very immature, then felt sad as she thought of the two of them, entrenched in that narrow home against the world with some mysterious background which could be felt but not fathomed.

Whatever the nature of the mystery surrounding the father, the boy knew nothing about it, for twice in Laura's presence he asked his mother, 'When will our Daddy come home?' and his mother, after a long pause, replied: 'Oh, not for a long time yet. He's travelling abroad, you know, and his gentleman's not ready to come home.' The first time she added, 'I expect they're shooting tigers', and the next, 'It's a long way to Spain.'

Once Tommy, in all innocence, brought out and showed Laura his father's photograph. It was that of a handsome, flashy-looking man posing before the rustic-work background of a photographer's studio. A top-hat and gloves were carefully arranged on a little table beside him. Not a working man, evidently, and yet he did not look quite like a gentleman, thought Laura, but it was no business of hers, and when she saw Mrs Macey's pained look as she took away the photograph she was glad that she had barely glanced at it. . . .

The Candleford Green workers lived in better cottages and many of them were better paid than the Lark Rise people. They were not all of them farm labourers; there were skilled craftsmen amongst them, and some were employed to drive vans by the tradesmen there and in Candleford town. But wages for all kinds of work were low and life for most of them must have been a struggle.

The length of raised sidewalk before the temptingly dressed windows of the Stores was the favourite afternoon promenade of the women, with or without perambulators. There *The Rage* or *The Latest*, so ticketed, might be seen free of charge, and the purchase of a reel of cotton or a paper of pins gave the right of entry to a further display of fashions. On Sundays the two Misses Pratt displayed the cream of their stock upon their own persons in church. They were tall, thin young women with frizzy Alexandra fringes of straw-coloured hair, high cheek-bones and anaemic complexions which they touched up with rouge.

At the font they had been given the pretty, old-fashioned names of Prudence and Ruth, but for business purposes, as they explained, they had exchanged them for the more high-sounding and up-to-date ones of Pearl and Ruby. The new names passed into currency sooner than might have been expected, for few of their customers cared to offend them. They might have retaliated by passing off on the offender an unbecoming hat or by skimping the sleeves of a new Sunday gown. So, to their faces, they were 'Miss Pearl' and 'Miss Ruby', while, behind their backs, as often as not, it would be 'That Ruby Pratt, as she calls herself', or 'Pearl as ought to be Prudence'.

Miss Ruby ran the dressmaking department and Miss Pearl reigned in the millinery showroom. Both were accepted authorities upon what was being worn and the correct manner of wearing it. If any one in the village was planning a new summer outfit and was not sure of the style, she would say, 'I must ask the Miss Pratts,' and although some

of the resulting creations might have astonished leaders of fashion elsewhere, they were accepted by their customers as models. In Laura's time the Pratts' customers included the whole feminine population of the village, excepting those rich enough to buy elsewhere and those too poor to buy at all at first-hand.

They were good enough girls, enterprising, hard-working, and clever, and if Laura thought them conceited, that may have been because she had been told that Miss Pearl had said to a customer in the showroom that she wondered that Miss Lane had not been able to find some one more genteel than that little country girl to assist her in her office.

At the time of her marriage, it was said, their mother had been looked upon as an heiress, having not only inherited the Stores, then a plain draper's shop with rolls of calico and red flannel in the window, but also cottages and grazing land, bringing in rent, so it may be supposed she felt justified in marrying where her fancy led her. It led her to marriage with a smart young commercial traveller whose round had brought him to the shop periodically, and together they had introduced modern improvements.

When the new plate-glass windows had been put in, the dress-making and millinery departments established, and the shop renamed 'The Stores', the husband's efforts had ended, and for the rest of his life he had felt himself entitled to spend most of his waking hours in the bar parlour of the 'Golden Lion' laying down the law to other commercial gentlemen who had not done so well for themselves. 'There goes that old Pratt again, shaking like a leaf and as thin as a hurdle,' Miss Lane would say when taking her morning survey of the green from her window, and Laura, glancing up from her work, would see the thin figure in loud tweeds and white bowler hat making for the door of the inn and know, without looking at the clock, that it was exactly eleven. Some time during the day he would go home for a meal, then return to his own special seat in the bar parlour, where he would remain until closing time.

At home his wife grew old and shrivelled and complaining, while the girls grew up and shouldered the business, just in time to stop its decline. At the time Laura knew them their 'Ma', as her daughters called her, had become an invalid on whom they lavished the tenderest care, obtaining far-fetched dainties to tempt her appetite, filling her room with flowers, and staging there a private show of their latest novelties before they were displayed to the public. 'No. Not that one, please, Mrs Perkins,' Miss Pearl said to a customer in Laura's hearing one day. 'I'm ever so sorry, but it's the new fashion, only just come in, and Ma's not seen it yet. I'd take it upstairs now to show her, but she takes her little siesta at this hour. Well, if you really don't *mind* stepping round again in the morning . . .'

If, through absent-mindedness or a lost sense of direction, Pa wandered in his hat and coat into the showroom, he was gently but firmly led out by a seemingly playful daughter. 'Dear Papa!' Miss Pearl would exclaim. 'He does take such an interest. But come along, darling. Come with your own little Pearlie. Mind the step, now! Gently does it. What you want is a nice strong cup of tea.'

No wonder the Pratt girls looked, as some people said, as if they had the weight of the world on their shoulders. They must in reality have carried a biggish burden of trouble, and if they tried to hide it with a show of high spirits and simpering smiles, plus a little harmless pretension, that should have been put down to their credit. Human nature being what it is, their shifts and pretences only served to provoke a little mild amusement. But, by the time Laura went to live at Candleford Green the Pratts' was an old story, until, one summer morning, a first-class sensation was provided for the villagers by the news that Mr Pratt had disappeared.

He had left the inn at the usual time, closing time, but had never reached home. His daughters had sat up for him, gone after midnight to the 'Golden Lion' to

188

inquire, and then headed the search in the lanes in the early dawn, but there was still no trace, and the police were about, asking questions of early workmen. Would they circulate his photograph? Would there be a reward? And, above all, what had become of the man? 'Thin as he was, he couldn't have fallen down a crack, like!'

The search went on for days. Stationmasters were questioned, woods were searched foot by foot, wells and ponds were dragged, but no trace could be found of Mr Pratt, dead or alive.

Ruby and Pearl, their first grief abating, took counsel with friends as to whether or not to wear mourning. But, no, they decided. Poor Pa might yet return, and they compromised by appearing in church in lavender frocks with touches of mauve, half, or perhaps quarter, mourning. As time went on, the back door, which, so far, had been left on the latch at night in case of the return of the prodigal father, was again locked, and perhaps, when alone with Ma, they admitted with a sigh that all might be for the best.

But they had not heard the last of poor Pa. One morning, nearly a year later, when Miss Ruby had got up very early and, the maid still being in bed, had herself gone to the wood-shed for sticks to boil a kettle to make tea, she found her father peacefully sleeping on a bed of brushwood. Where he had been all those months he could not or would not say. He thought, or pretended to think, that there had been no interval of time, that he had come home as usual from the 'Golden Lion' the night before he was found and, finding the door locked and not liking to disturb the household, had retired to the woodshed. The one and only clue to the mystery, and that did not solve it, was that in the early dawn of the day before that of his reappearance a cyclist on the Oxford road, a few miles out of that city, had passed on the road a tall, thin elderly man in a deerstalker cap walking with his head bent and sobbing.

Where he had been and how he had managed to live while he was away was never found out. He resumed his visits to the 'Golden Lion' and his daughters shouldered their burden again. By them the episode was always afterwards referred to as 'Poor Pa's loss of memory'. . . .

But we must return to the Post Office, where Laura in the course of her duties was to come to know almost every one.

— XII —

AT THE POST OFFICE

SOMETIMES Sir Timothy would come in, breathing heavily and mopping his brow if the weather were warm. 'Ha! ha!' he would say. 'Here is our future Postmistress-General. What is the charge for a telegram of thirty-three words to Timbuctu? Ah! I thought so. You don't know without looking it up in a book, so I'll send it to Oxford instead and hope you'll be better informed next time I ask you. There! Can you read my handwriting? I'm dashed if I can always read it myself. Well, well. Your eyes are young. Let's hope they'll never be dimmed with crying, eh, Miss Lane? And I see you are looking as young and handsome as ever yourself. Do you remember that afternoon I caught you picking cowslips in Godstone Spinney? Trespassing, you were, trespassing; and I very properly fined you on the spot, although not as yet a J.P. – not by many a year. I let you off lightly that time, though you made such a fuss about a mere –'

'Oh, Sir Timothy, how you do rake up things! And I wasn't trespassing, as you very well knew; it was a footpath your father ought never to have closed.'

'But the game birds, woman, the game birds –' And, if no one else happened to come in, they would talk on of their youth.

For Lady Adelaide, Sir Timothy's wife, the footman usually did business while she sat in her carriage outside, but occasionally she herself would come rustling in, bringing with her a whiff of perfume, and sink languidly down in the chair provided for customers on their side of the counter. She was a graceful woman, and it was a delight to watch her movements. Laura, who sat behind her in church, admired the way she knelt for the prayers, not plumping down squarely with one boot-sole on each side of a substantial posterior, as most other women of her age did, but slanting gracefully forward with the sole of one dainty shoe in advance of the other. She was tall and thin and, Laura thought, aristocratic-looking.

For some time she took no more notice of Laura than one would now of an automatic stamp-delivering machine. Then, one day, she did her the honour of personally inviting her to join the Primrose League, of which she was a Dame and the chief local patroness. A huge fête, in which branches from the surrounding villages joined, was held in Sir Timothy's park every midsummer, and there were day excursions and winter-evening entertainments for the benefit of Primrose League members. It was no wonder the pretty little enamelled primrose badge, worn as a brooch or lapel ornament, was so much in evidence at church on Sundays.

But Laura hesitated and grew red as a peony. In view of her Ladyship's graciousness, it seemed churlish to refuse to join; but what would her father, a declared Liberal in politics and an opponent of all that the Primrose League stood for, say if she went over to the enemy?

And she herself did not really wish to become a member; she never did wish to do what everybody else was doing, which showed she had a contrary nature, she had often been told, but it was really because her thoughts and tastes ran upon different lines than those of the majority.

The lady looked her in the face, her expression showing more interest than formerly. Perhaps she noticed her embarrassment, and Laura, who admired her sincerely and wanted to be liked by her, was about to cave in when 'Dare to be a Daniel!' said an inward voice. It was a catchword of the moment derived from the Salvation Army hymn, 'Dare to be a Daniel. Dare to stand alone', and was more often used as a laughing excuse for refusing a glass of beer in company or adopting a new style of hairdressing than seriously as a support to conscience; but it served.

'But we are Liberals at home,' said Laura apologetically, and, at that, the lady smiled and said kindly: 'Well, in that case, you had better ask your parents' permission before joining,' and that was the end of the matter as far as she was concerned. But it was a landmark in Laura's mental development. Afterwards she laughed at herself for daring to be a Daniel on so small a matter. The mighty Primrose League, with its overwhelming membership, was certainly not in need of another small member. Her Ladyship, she realized, had asked her to join out of kindness, in order that she might qualify for a ticket for the approaching celebrations, and had probably already forgotten the episode. It was better to say clearly and simply just what one meant, whoever one was talking to, and always to remember that what one said was probably of no importance whatever to one's listener. . . .

One day a man known as 'Long Bob', a lock-keeper on the canal, came in with a small package which he wished to send by registered post. It was roughly done up in soiled brown paper, and the string, although much knotted, was minus the wax seals required by the regulations. When Laura offered him the loan of the office sealing-wax, he asked her to seal and make tidy the package for him, saying that his fingers were all thumbs and he hadn't got no 'ooman now to do such fiddling little jobs for him. 'But maybe,' he added, 'before you start on it, you'd like to have a look at that within.'

He then opened the package and brought forth and shook out a panel of coloured embroidery. It was a needlework picture of Adam and Eve, standing one on each side of the Tree of Knowledge with a grove of flowering and fruiting trees behind them and a lamb, a rabbit, and other small creatures in the foreground. It was exquisitely executed and the colours, though faded in places, were beautifully blended. The hair of Adam and Eve was embroidered with real human hair and the fur of the furry animals of some woolly substance. That it was very old even the inexperienced Laura could sense at the first glance, more by something strange and antique-looking about the nude human figures and the shape of the trees than by any visible sign of wear or decay in the fabric. 'It's very old, isn't it?' she asked, expecting Long Bob to say it had belonged to his grandmother.

'Very old and ancient indeed,' he replied, 'and I'm told there's some clever men in London who'll like to see that pictur'. All done by hand, they say, oh, long agone, before old Queen Bess's day.' Then, seeing Laura all eyes and ears, he told her how it had come into his possession.

About a year before, it appeared, he had found the panel on the towing-path of the canal, carelessly screwed up in a sheet of newspaper. Inspired rather by strict principles of honesty than by any idea that the panel was valuable, he had taken it to the Police Station at Candleford, where the sergeant in charge had asked him to leave it while inquiries were made. It had then, apparently, been examined by experts, for the next thing Long Bob heard from the police was that the panel was old and valuable and that inquiries as to its ownership were in progress. It was thought that it must have been part of the proceeds of some burglary. But there had been no burglary in that part of the county for several years, and the police could get no information of any more distant one where such an article was missing. The owner was never found, and, at the end of the time appointed by law, the panel was handed back to the finder, together with the address of a London sale-room to which he was advised to send it. A few weeks later he received the, to him, large sum of five pounds which its sale had realized.

That was the recent history of the needlework panel. What of its past? How had it come to lie, wrapped in a fairly recent newspaper, on the canal tow-path that foggy November morning?

Nobody ever knew. Miss Lane and Laura thought that by some means it had come into the possession of a cottage family, which, though ignorant of its value, had treasured it as a curiosity. Then, perhaps, it may have been sent by a child as a present to some relative, or as part of an inheritance from some old grandmother who had recently died. The loss by a child of 'that old sampler of Granny's' would be but a matter of cuffing and scolding; poor people would not dream of making what they called a 'hue and cry' about such a loss, or of going to the police. But this was mere supposition; the ownership of the panel and how it came to be found in such an unlikely place remained a mystery. . . .

Friends and acquaintances who came to the Post Office used often to say to Laura: 'How dull it must be for you here.' But although she sometimes agreed mildly for the sake of not appearing peculiar, Laura did not find life at the Post Office at all dull. She was so young and new to life that small things which older people might not have noticed surprised and pleased her. All day interesting people were coming in –

interesting to her, at least – and if there were intervals between these callers, there was always something waiting to be done. Sometimes, in a few spare moments, Miss Lane would come in and find her reading a book from the parlour or the Mechanics' Institute. Although she had not actually forbidden reading for pleasure on duty, she did not altogether approve of it, for she thought it looked unbusinesslike. So she would say, rather acidly: 'Are you sure you can learn nothing more from the Rule Book?' and Laura would once more take down from its shelf the large, cream, cardboard-bound tome she had already studied until she knew many of the rules word for word. From even that dry-as-dust reading she extracted some pleasure. On one page, for instance, set in a paragraph composed of stiff, official phrases, was the word 'mignonette'. It referred only to the colour of a form, or something of that kind, but to Laura it seemed like a pressed flower, still faintly scented. . . .

The sound of a bicycle being propped against the wall outside was less frequent than that of a horse's hoofs; but there were already a few cyclists, and the number of these increased rapidly when the new low safety bicycle superseded the old penny-farthing type. Then, sometimes, on a Saturday afternoon, the call of a bugle would be heard, followed by the scuffling of dismounting feet, and a stream of laughing, jostling young men would press into the tiny office to send facetious telegrams. These members of the earliest cycling clubs had a great sense of their own importance, and dressed up to their part in a uniform composed of a tight navy knicker-bocker suit with red or yellow braided coat and a small navy pill-box cap embroidered with their club badge. The leader carried a bugle suspended on a coloured cord from his shoulder. Cycling was considered such a dangerous pastime that they telegraphed home news of their safe arrival at the farthest point in their journey. Or perhaps they sent the telegrams to prove how far they really had travelled, for a cyclist's word as to his day's mileage then ranked with an angler's account of his catch.

'Did run in two hours, forty and a half minutes. Only ran down two fowls, a pig, and a carter', is a fair sample of their communications. The bag was mere brag; the senders had probably hurt no living creature; some of them may even have dismounted by the roadside to allow a horsed carriage to pass, but every one of them liked to pose as 'a regular devil of a fellow'.

They were townsmen out for a lark, and, after partaking of refreshment at the hotel, they would play leap-frog or kick an old tin about the green. They had a lingo of their own. Quite common things, according to them, were 'scrumptious', or 'awfully good', or 'awfully rotten', or just 'bally awful'. Cigarettes they called 'fags'; their bicycles their 'mounts', or 'my machine' or 'my trusty steed'; the Candleford Green people they alluded to as 'the natives'. Laura was addressed by them as 'fair damsel', and their favourite ejaculation was 'What ho!' or 'What ho, she bumps!'

But they were not to retain their position as bold pioneer adventurers long. Soon, every man, youth and boy whose families were above the poverty line was riding a bicycle. For some obscure reason, the male sex tried hard to keep the privilege of bicycle riding to themselves. If a man saw or heard of a woman riding he was horrified. 'Unwomanly. Most unwomanly! God knows what the world's coming to,' he would say; but, excepting the fat and elderly and the sour and envious, the women suspended judgement. They saw possibilities which they were soon to seize. The wife of a doctor in Candleford town was the first woman cyclist in that district. 'I should like to tear her off that thing and smack her pretty little backside,' said one old man, grinding his teeth with fury. One of more gentle character sighed and said: "T'ood break my heart if I saw my wife on one of they,'

which those acquainted with the figure of his middle-aged wife thought reasonable.

Their protestations were unavailing; one woman after another appeared riding a glittering new bicycle. In long skirts, it is true, but with most of their petticoats left in the bedroom behind them. Even those women who as yet did not cycle gained something in freedom of movement, for the two or three bulky petticoats formerly worn were replaced by neat serge knickers – heavy and cumbersome knickers, compared with those of today, with many buttons and stiff buttonholes and cambric linings to be sewn in on Saturday nights, but a great improvement on the petticoats.

And oh! the joy of the new means of progression. To cleave the air as though on wings, defying time and space by putting what had been a day's journey on foot behind one in a couple of hours! Of passing garrulous acquaintances who had formerly held one in one-sided conversation by the roadside for an hour, with a light *ting, ting* of the

bell and a casual wave of recognition.

At first only comparatively well-to-do women rode bicycles; but soon almost everyone under forty was awheel, for those who could not afford to buy a bicycle could hire one for sixpence an hour. The men's shocked criticism petered out before the *fait accompli*, and they contented themselves with such mild thrusts as:

> *Mother's out upon her bike, enjoying of the fun,*
> *Sister and her beau have gone to take a little run.*
> *The housemaid and the cook are both a-riding on their wheels;*
> *And Daddy's in the kitchen a-cooking of the meals.*

And very good for Daddy it was. He had had all the fun hitherto; now it was his wife's and daughter's turn. The knell of the selfish, much-waited-upon, old-fashioned father of the family was sounded by the bicycle bell. . . .

One cold winter morning, when snow was on the ground and the ponds were iced over, Laura, in mittens and a scarf, was sorting the early morning mail and wishing that Zillah would hurry with the cup of tea she usually brought her at that time. The hanging oil lamp above her head had scarcely had time to thaw the atmosphere, and the one uniformed postman at a side bench, sorting his letters for delivery, stopped to thump his chest with his arms and exclaim that he'd be jiggered, but it was a fact that on such mornings as this there was bound to be a letter for every house, even for those which did not have one once in a blue moon. 'Does it on purpose, I s'pose,' he grumbled.

The two women letter-carriers, who had more reason than he to complain, for his round was mostly by road and theirs were cross-country, worked quietly at their bench. The elder, Mrs Gubbins, had got herself up to face the weather by tying a red knitted shawl over her head and wearing the bottoms of a man's corduroy trouser-legs as gaiters. Mrs Macey had brought out an old, moth-eaten fur tippet which smelt strongly of camphor. As the daylight increased, the window became a steely grey square with wads of snow at the corners of the panes. From beyond it came the crunching sound of cart-wheels on frozen snow. Laura turned back her mittens and rubbed her chilblains.

Then, suddenly, the everyday dullness of work before breakfast was pierced by a low cry of distress from the younger postwoman. She had an open letter in her hand and evidently it contained bad news, but all she would say in answer to sympathetic inquiries was: 'I must go. I must go at once. Now, immediately.' Go at once? Go where? And why? How could she go anywhere but on her round? Or leave her letters half-sorted? were the shocked questions the eyes of the other three asked each other. When Laura suggested calling Miss Lane, Mrs Macey exclaimed: 'No, don't call her here, please. I must see her alone and in private. And I shan't be able to take out the letters this morning. Oh, dear! Oh, dear! What's to be done?'

Miss Lane was downstairs and alone in the kitchen, with her feet on the fender, sipping a cup of tea. Laura had expected she would be annoyed at being disturbed before her official hours, but she did not even seem to be surprised, and in a few moments had Mrs Macey in a chair by the fire and was holding a cup of hot tea to her lips. 'Come. Drink this,' she said. 'Then tell me about it.' Then to Laura, who had

already reached the door on her way back to her sorting, 'Tell Zillah not to begin cooking breakfast until I tell her to,' and, as an after-thought: 'Say she is to go upstairs and begin getting my room ready for turning out,' a message which, when delivered, annoyed Zillah exceedingly, for she knew and she knew Laura would guess that the upstairs work was ordered to prevent listening at keyholes.

The sorting was finished, the postman had gone reluctantly out, five minutes late, and old Mrs Gubbins was pretending to hunt for a lost piece of string in order to delay her own exit when Miss Lane came in and carefully shut the door after her. 'What? Not out yet, Mrs Gubbins?' she asked coldly, and Mrs Gubbins responded to the hint, banging the door behind her as the only possible expression of her frustrated curiosity.

'Here's a pretty kettle of fish! We're in a bit of a fix, Laura. Mrs Macey won't be able to do her round this morning. She's got to go off by train at once to see her husband, who's dangerously ill. She's gone home now to get Tommy up and get ready. She's taking him with her.'

'But I thought her husband was abroad,' said the puzzled Laura.

'So he may have been at one time, but he isn't now. He's down in Devonshire, and it'll take her all day to get there, and a cold, miserable journey it'll be for the poor soul. But I'll tell you more about that later. The thing now is what we are going to do about the letters and Sir Timothy's private postbag. Zillah shan't go. I wouldn't demean myself to ask her, after the disgraceful way she's been banging about upstairs, not to mention her bad feet and her rheumatism. And Minnie's got a bad cold. She couldn't take out the telegrams yesterday, as you know, and nobody can be spared from the forge with this frost, and horses pouring in to be rough-shod; and every moment it's getting later, and you know what old Farmer Stebbing is: if his letters are ten minutes late, he writes off to the Postmaster-General, though, to be sure, he might make some small allowance this morning for snow and late mails. What a fool I must have been to take on this office. It's nothing but worry, worry, worry –'

'And I suppose I couldn't be spared to go?' asked Laura tentatively. Miss Lane was inclined to reconsider things if she appeared too eager. But now, to her great delight, that lady said, quite gratefully, 'Oh, *would* you? And you don't think your mother would mind? Well, that's a weight off my mind! But you're not going without some breakfast inside you, time or no time, or for all the farmers and squires in creation.' Then, opening the door: 'Zillah! Zillah! Laura's breakfast at once! And bring plenty. She's going out on an errand for me. Bacon and two eggs, and make haste, please.' And Laura ate her breakfast and dressed herself in her warmest clothes, with the addition of a sealskin cap and tippet Miss Lane insisted upon lending her, and hurried out into the snowy world, a hind let loose, if ever there was one.

As soon as she had left the village behind, she ran, kicking up the snow and sliding along the puddles, and managed to reach Farmer Stebbing's house only a little later than the time appointed for the delivery of his letters in the ordinary way by the post-office authorities. Then across the park to Sir Timothy's mansion and on to his head gardener's house and the home farm and half a dozen cottages, and her letters were disposed of.

Laura never forgot that morning's walk. Fifty years later she could recall it in detail. Snow had fallen a few days earlier, then had frozen, and on the hard crust yet more snow had fallen and lay like soft, feathery down, fleecing the surface of the level open spaces of the park and softening the outlines of hillocks and fences. Against it the dark branches and twigs of the trees stood out, lacelike. The sky was low and grey and soft-looking as a feather-bed. . . .

In spite of a late start and a leisurely return, Laura managed to reach the office only a few minutes later than the official time fixed for that journey, which pleased Miss

Lane, as it saved her the trouble of making a report, and that, perhaps, made her more communicative than usual, for, at the first opportunity, she told Laura what she knew of Mrs Macey's story.

Her husband, Laura now learned, was not a valet, although he might at one time have been one; nor was he travelling with his gentleman. He was by profession a bookmaker, which interested Laura greatly, as she at first concluded that he was in some way engaged in the production of literature. But Miss Lane, who knew more of the world, made haste to explain that his kind of bookmaker had something to do with betting on race-horses. In the course of his bookmaking, she said, he had been involved in a public-house quarrel which had led to blows, and from blows to kicks, and a man had been killed. The crime had been brought home to him and he had been given a long sentence for manslaughter. Now he was in prison on Dartmoor, nearing the end of his sentence. A long, long way for that poor soul to go in that wintry weather;

but the prison authorities had written to say he was dangerously ill with pneumonia and the prison doctor thought it advisable that his wife should be sent for.

Miss Lane had known all the time where he was, though not what crime had caused him to be there, and she had not breathed a word to a living soul, she assured Laura, and would not be doing so now had not Mrs Macey said, as she went out of the door: 'Perhaps Laura will go over and feed Snowball. I'll pay for his milk when I get back. And tell her whatever you think fit about where we are going. She's a sensible little soul and won't tell anybody if you ask her not to.'

Poor Mrs Macey! No wonder she had been distressed. The strain of the journey in such weather and the ordeal at the end of it were not the whole of her trouble. As far as Tommy knew, his father was a gentleman's servant travelling abroad with his employer. Now, at some point on their journey, she would have to tell him the truth and to prepare him for whatever might follow. . . .

A week later, Mrs Macey returned, sad and subdued, but not in mourning, as Miss Lane had half-expected. She had spent a night in London and left Tommy with her friends there, for she had only come back to settle up her small affairs and to pack her furniture. Her husband was recovering and would shortly be released, and she had decided to make a home for him, for a husband is a husband, as Miss Lane had so sagely remarked, and although Mrs Macey obviously dreaded the future, she felt she must face it. But she could not let her husband come to Candleford Green to make a nine days' wonder. She would find a couple of rooms near her friends in London, and the Prisoners' Aid people would find him a job, or if not, she could earn their keep with her needle. She was sorry to leave her nice little cottage – she had had a few years' peace there – but, as Laura would find, you can't always do what you like or be where you would wish in this world.

So she went with her boxes and bundles and with Snowball mewing in a basket. Someone else came to live in her cottage and very soon she was forgotten, as Laura, in her turn, would be forgotten, and as all the other insignificant people would be who had sojourned for a time at Candleford Green.

But her going had its effect upon Laura's life, for, after a good deal of discussion among her elders and hopes and fears on Laura's part, it was arranged that she should undertake what was still known as 'Mrs Macey's delivery'. Miss Lane was quite willing to spare her for two and a half hours each morning. She had suggested the plan, pointing out it would not only give her more fresh air and exercise, but also put another four shillings a week in her pocket.

It was really most generous of Miss Lane; and four shillings a week was considered quite a substantial addition to larger incomes than Laura's in those days; yet Laura, sent home for a week-end to obtain her parents' consent to the arrangement found them less pleased with the plan than she had expected. Except in letters from Laura, neither of them had heard of postwomen before, and the idea of letters being delivered by any one but a man in uniform struck them as odd. Her father thought she would demean herself and get coarse and tomboyish trapesing about the country with a letterbag strapped over her shoulder. Her mother's objection was that people would think it funny. However, as it was Miss Lane's suggestion and Laura herself was bent on the plan, they gave, at last, a grudging consent, her father stipulating that she should keep strictly to her official timetable and favour nobody, and her mother that she should never forget to change her shoes in wet weather. . . .

The official time allowance for the journey was so generous that she found that, by walking quickly on her outward way, she could deliver her letters and still have an hour to spare for sauntering and exploring before she need hurry back home. The scheme had evidently been drawn up for older and more sedate travellers than Laura.

Soon she came to know every tree, flower-patch and fern-clump beside her path, as well as the gardens, houses, and faces of the people on her round. There was the head gardener's cottage, semi-Gothic and substantial against the glittering range of glasshouses, and his witty, talkative Welsh wife, kindly, but difficult to escape from; and the dairymaid at the farmhouse who had orders to give her a mug of milk every morning and see that she drank it, because the farmer's wife thought she was growing beyond her strength; and the row of half a dozen cottages, all exactly alike in outward appearance and inside accommodation, but differing in their degree of comfort and cleanliness. Laura wondered then, as she was often to do in her after-life, why, with houses exactly alike and incomes the same to a penny, one woman will have a cosy, tasteful little home and another something not much better than a slum dwelling.

The women at the cottages, clean and not so clean alike, were always pleasant to Laura, especially when she brought them the letters they were always longing for, but seldom received. On many mornings she did not have to go to the cottages, for there was not a letter for any one there, and this left her with still more time to loiter by the pond, reaching out over the water for brandyballs, as the small yellow water-lily was called there, or to brood with her hand over bird's eggs in a nest, or to blow dandelion clocks in the sun. Her uniform in summer was a clean print frock and a shady straw hat, which she would sometimes trim with a wreath of living wild flowers. In wet weather she wore her stout new shoes and a dark purplish waterproof cloak, presented to her by one of her Candleford aunts. She carried a postman's pouch over her shoulder and, for the first part of her outward journey, Sir Timothy's locked leather private postbag.

The only drawbacks to perfect happiness on her part were footmen and cows. The cows would crowd round the stiles she had to get over and be deaf to all her mild shooings. She had been used to cows all her life and had no fear of them in the open, but the idea of descending from the stile into that sea of heads and horns was alarming. She knew they were gentle creatures and would never attack her; but, accidentally, perhaps –. Their horns were so very sharp and long. Then, one morning, a cowman saw her hesitating and bade her, 'Coom on.' If she approached and climbed over the stile quickly, he said the cows would disperse. 'They dunno what you want to be up to. Let 'em see that you've got business on the other side of that stile and that you be in a hurry and they'll make way for 'ee. They be knowin' old craturs, cows.' It was as he had said: when she came to and crossed the stile in a businesslike way, they moved politely aside for her to pass, and they soon became so used to seeing her there that they dispersed at her approach.

The footmen were far less mannerly. At the hour at which she reached the great house every morning, their duties, or their pleasure, lay in the back premises, near the door at which Sir Timothy's postbag had to be delivered. At the sound of the doorbell, two or three of them would rush out, snatch the leather postbag from Laura's hand and toss it from one to the other – sometimes kick it. They hated that postbag because their own private letters were locked therein, and if Sir Timothy was out on the estate or engaged in his Justice Room, they had to wait until he was ready, or chose, to unlock it. They accused him of examining the handwriting and postmarks of their correspondence and of asking inquisitive questions about it. Which he may at some time have done, for, in Laura's time, they had betting tips and bookmakers' circulars addressed to the Post Office to be called for.

It was this matter of the postbag which had caused their animosity towards Laura. When she had first appeared as postwoman they had asked – or, rather, told – her to bring up to the house with the bag their letters addressed to the Post Office. Miss Lane, who was a stickler for strict observance of the official rules, would not permit her to do this. If a letter was addressed to the Post Office to be called for, she said, called for it must be, and although Laura, who thought it unfair that their letters should be inspected, like those of small boys at school, had softened Miss Lane's message to them when delivering it, they were annoyed and under a show of boisterous horseplay visited their annoyance upon Laura.

They would creep silently up behind her and clap her heavily upon the shoulders, or

knock her hat over her eyes, or ruffle her hair with their hands, or try to kiss her. The maids, several of whom were often present, as the house-keeper and the butler were at that time taking their morning coffee in the housekeeper's room, would only laugh at her discomfiture, or join in the sport, putting pebbles down her neck, or flicking her face with their dusting-brushes.

'You look as if you'd been drawn through a quickset hedge backward,' remarked the head gardener's wife one day when Laura was more than usually dishevelled; but, when told what had happened, she only laughed and said: 'Well, you're only young once. You must get all the fun you can. You give them as good as they give you and they'll soon learn to respect you.' She dared not tell Miss Lane, for she knew that lady would complain to Sir Timothy and there would be what she thought of as 'a fuss'. She preferred to endure the teasing, which, after all, occupied but a few minutes during an outing in which there were rich compensations.

Excepting the men working in the fields, she seldom saw any one between the houses on her round. Now and then she would meet the estate carpenter with his bag of tools, going to mend a fence or a gate, and occasionally she saw Sir Timothy himself, spud in hand, taking what he called 'a toddle round the estate', and he would greet her in his jovial way as 'our little Postmistress-General' and tell her to go to Geering, the head gardener, and ask him to show her through the glasshouses and give her some flowers. Which was kind of him, but unnecessary, as Mr Geering had, on his own responsibility, conducted her several times through the long, warm, damp, scented hothouses, picking a flower here and there to add to her bouquet. *My* glasshouses, the gardener called them; *our* glasshouses, said his wife when speaking of them; to the actual owner they were merely *the* glasshouses. So much for the privilege of ownership!

Once she saw Sir Timothy in a more serious mood. That was after a night of high wind had brought down two magnificent elm trees on the edge of the ha-ha, and he called to her to come and look at the damage. It was a sad sight. The trees were lying with their roots upended and their trunks slanting across the ditch to the ruin of broken branches and smashed twigs on the lower level. Sir Timothy appeared to be as much distressed as if they had been the only trees he possessed. There were tears in his eyes as he kept repeating: 'Wouldn't have lost them for worlds! Known them all my life. Opened my eyes upon them, in fact, for I was born in that room there. See the window? It's this damned sunk fence is to blame. No root room on one side. Wouldn't have lost them for worlds!' And she left him lamenting.

Although so few people were seen there at the early hour of Laura's passing, the park was open to all. Couples went there for walks on summer Sundays, and the poorer villagers were permitted to pick up the dead fallen wood for their fires; but the copses and other enclosures were barred, especially in the spring, when the game birds were nesting. There were notice boards in such places to say trespassers would be prosecuted and, although Laura considered herself to some extent a privileged person, she climbed into them stealthily and kept a lookout for the gamekeeper. But he was an old man, getting beyond his work, people said; his cottage stood in a clearing in a wood on the other side of the estate, and she never once sighted him.

She went in and out of the copses, gathering bluebells or wild cherry blossom, or hunting for birds' nests, and never saw anyone, until one May morning of her second year on the round. She had gone into one of the copses where a few lilies-of-the-valley grew wild, found half a dozen or so, and was just climbing down the high bank which surrounded the copse when she came face to face with a stranger. He was a young man in rough country tweeds and carried a gun over his shoulder. She thought for a moment that he might be one of Sir Timothy's nephews, or some other visitor at the great house, though, of course, she should have remembered that no guest of Sir Timothy's would have carried a gun at that season. But, when he pointed to a notice board which said *Trespassers will be prosecuted* and asked, rather roughly, what the devil she thought she was doing there, she knew he must be a gamekeeper, and he turned out to be a new underkeeper engaged to do most of the actual work of the old man, who was failing in health, but refused to retire.

He was a tall, well-built young man, apparently in the middle twenties, with a small fair moustache and very pale blue eyes which, against his dark tanned complexion, looked paler. His features might have been called handsome but for their set rigidity. These softened slightly when Laura held out her half-dozen lilies-of-the-valley as an excuse for her trespass. He was sure she had meant to do no harm, he said, but the pheasants were still sitting and he could not have them disturbed. There had been too much of this trespassing lately – Laura wondered by whom – too much laxity, too much laxity, he repeated, as if he had just thought of the word and was pleased with it, but it had got to stop. Then, still walking close on her heels on the narrow path, as if to keep her in custody, he asked her if she would tell him the way to Foxhill Copse, as it was his first morning on the estate and he had not grasped the lie of the land yet. When she pointed it out and he saw that her own path led past, he unbent sufficiently to suggest that they should walk on together.

By the time they reached the copse he had become quite human. His name, he told her, was Philip White. His father was head gamekeeper on an estate near Oxford and he had so far worked under him, but had now come to Candleford Park on the understanding that when poor old Chitty died or retired he would take his place as head gamekeeper. Without actually saying so, he managed to convey the impression that by consenting to serve under Chitty for a time he was doing, not only Sir Timothy, but the whole neighbourhood a favour. His father's estate (he spoke of it as his father's in the way the Geerings spoke of 'our glasshouses') was larger and better preserved than this, and belonged to a very great nobleman with an historic title. He did not claim the title as a family possession, but it was evident that he felt its reflected glory.

Laura glanced up at him. No. He was perfectly serious. There was no smile on his face, not even a twinkle in his pale eyes; the only expression there was one of a faint interest in herself. Before they parted she had been shown a photograph of his sister, who worked in a draper's showroom in Oxford. It was that of a smiling girl in evening dress for some dance, with her fair hair dressed in curls high on her head. Laura was much impressed. 'All in our family are good-looking,' he said as he slipped the photograph back into his breast pocket. She had also been given a description of his parents' model cottage on the famous estate and been told of the owner's great shoots, to which dukes and lords and millionaires appeared to flock, and would probably have heard much more had not her conscience pricked her into saying: 'I really must go now, or I shall have to run all the way.' She had not told him anything about herself, nor had he asked any questions beyond inquiring where she lived and how often she passed that way. Happening to look back as she climbed over the stile, she saw him still standing where she had left him. He raised his hand in a wooden salute, and that, she thought, was the last she would see of him.

But she had not seen the last of Philip White. After that he always seemed to appear at some point on her walk. At first he would spring out of some copse with his gun and seem to be surprised to see her; but soon he would stroll openly along the path to meet her, then turn and walk by her side through the park until just before they came in sight of the great house windows. Beyond telling Miss Lane as an item of news on

the first morning that a new under-keeper had come and that he had asked her the way to Fox'lls, Laura mentioned these meetings to no one, and as they met on the loneliest part of her round no one she knew ever saw them together. But for weeks they met almost daily and talked, or rather Philip talked and she listened. Sometimes he would take the hand which swung by her side and hold it in his as they walked on together. It was pleasant at sixteen to be the object of so much attention on the part of a grown man and from one who was spoken of respectfully by the villagers as Keeper White, while to her in secret he was Philip. 'Call me Philip,' he had said at their second meeting. 'I wouldn't allow any one else here to call me it, but I'd like it from you,' and she called him by that name occasionally. Never 'Phil'; it would not have suited him. He called her 'Laura', and once or twice when they passed through the kissing gate, he gave her a shy, cold, wooden kind of kiss over the bars.

She supposed they were sweethearts and sometimes looked into the future and saw herself feeding the pheasant chicks hatched out under hens in the little coops under the green clearing where old Chitty's cottage stood. She felt she could be happy for life in that pretty cottage on the green, surrounded by waving tree-tops. On one of her walks last spring she had seen the margins of the green and the earth under the trees starred with white wild anenomes, swaying in the wind, and it had looked to her then a perfect paradise. But then came the dampening thought that Philip would be there, too, at least some of the time, and she was not sure that she liked Philip well enough to be able to endure his perpetual company.

He was so self-satisfied, so sure that he and everything and everybody belonging to him were perfect, and he had no interests whatever outside his own affairs. If she tried to talk about other people or of flowers she had found, or some book she was reading, it was never long before he brought the conversation back to himself again. 'That's like *me,*' he would say, or, 'What *I* think about it is –' or, '*I* couldn't stand that sort of thing,' and she, who loved to listen to most people and found nearly everybody else interesting, wanted to run straight away across the park and fields and leave him talking to himself. . . .

Then, when she least expected it, the whole affair came to a head and was over. It was just upon closing time one evening, and she had taken some forms to Miss Lane, who was already seated at the kitchen table about to begin on her accounts, when the office doorbell tinkled and she hurried back to find Philip there. That, to begin with, was a surprise to her, for he had never been in the office before – an embarrassment, too, for she knew that Miss Lane, sitting quietly at the kitchen table with the door wide open, would hear every word that was said. But there he was, looking full of importance, and all she could do to cope with the situation was to say 'Good evening' in what

she hoped was a businesslike voice. She almost prayed that he would say, 'Three penny stamps' or something of that kind and go. He might squeeze her hand, if he liked; she did not care if he kissed her, if only he kissed her quietly and Miss Lane did not hear. But she was not to be let off so easily.

Without any formal greeting, he pulled a letter out of his pocket and said: 'Can you get off for a few days at the end of this week? Well, as a matter of fact, you must. I've got this letter from our Cath' – his sister – 'and she says our Mum says I'm to bring you. Saturday to Monday, she says, or longer if we can manage it, but, of course, I can't. Nobody can afford to leave my job for long together – too many bad characters about. Still, I think I have earned a day or two and Sir Timothy's quite agreeable, so you'd better arrange about it now and I'll wait.'

Laura looked at the open door; she could positively feel Miss Lane listening. 'I'm s-s-sorry –' she began feebly, but the idea of any one trying to refuse an invitation from his family was unthinkable to Philip. 'Go and ask,' he commanded; then, more gently, but still too, too audibly: 'Go and ask. You've got the right. Everybody takes their girl for their people to see; and you are my girl, aren't you, Laura?'

The papers on the kitchen table rustled, then again dead silence, but Laura was no longer thinking of the danger of being overheard so much as wondering what she should say.

'You are my girl, aren't you, Laura?' asked Philip once more, and for the first time since she had known him, Laura detected a faint note of uneasiness in his voice. She herself was trembling with consternation, but when she said, 'You've never asked me,' her voice sounded flippant, perhaps coquettish, for Philip took one of her trembling hands and smiled down upon her as he said magnanimously: 'Well, I thought you understood. But don't be frightened. You will be my girl. Won't you Laura?' That was inadequate enough as a declaration of love, but Laura's answer was even more inadequate: 'No – no thank you, Philip,' she said, and the most unromantic love scene on record was over, for, without another word, he turned, went out of the door and out of her life. She never saw him again to speak to. On one occasion, months afterwards, she had a momentary view of his distant figure, gun on shoulder, stalking across one of the open spaces of the park, but, if he ever came her way again, he must have chosen a time of day when she was not likely to be there. . . .

In after years Laura sometimes looked rather wistfully back on that evening when an apparent choice was offered her between two widely differing paths in life. It would have been pleasant to have lived all her days in comparative ease and security among the people she knew and understood. To have watched the seasons open and fade in the scenes she loved and belonged to by birth. But have we any of us a free choice of our path in life, or are we driven on by destiny or by the demon within us into a path already marked out? Who can tell?

Choice or no choice, Laura's sojourn at Candleford Green was to be but of a few years' duration. And, if the choice had been hers and she had remained there, her life might not have been as happy and peaceful as she afterwards imagined it would have been. Her mother's judgement was usually sound, and she had often told her: 'You're not cut out for a pleasant, easy life. You think too much!' Sometimes adding tolerantly: 'But we are as we are made, I suppose.'

—— XIII ——
CHANGE IN THE VILLAGE

ABOUT that time came a rise in wages. Agricultural workers were given fifteen instead of ten or twelve shillings a week, and skilled craftsmen were paid an agreed rate per hour, instead of the former weekly wage irrespective of the time put in, and although at the same time prices were rising, they had not as yet risen in proportion. The Boer War, when it came, sent prices soaring, but that was still several years in the future.

Meanwhile, Queen Victoria had her Diamond Jubilee and 'Peace and Plenty' was the country's watchword. Rural councils were established and some of the progressive Candleford Green villagers were able to voice their improvement schemes and to get a few of them carried out. There were rumours of scholarships for village schoolchildren; the County Council sent a cookery expert to lecture in the schoolroom; and there were evening classes, no longer called 'night school', for the older boys. Housing was still left to private enterprise, but the demand for more modern homes did not go unregarded.

When one of the Candleford Green villagers had a stroke of good luck in the way of a better job or higher wages, his wife's reaction to the good news would usually be to exclaim: 'Now we can go to live in one of the villas!' Sometimes her ambition was realized and they exchanged their old, inconvenient, though thick-walled and warm old cottage with its large, fertile garden for one of a row of small houses on the newly opened building estate on the Candleford Road.

The new house might prove to be damp and draughty, for the walls were thin and the woodwork ill-fitted, and the garden at the back of the house, formerly part of a damp, tussocky meadow, left in the rough by the builder, would certainly turn out what her husband would call 'a heartache'; but, as compensation, she would enjoy the distinction conferred by owning a smart front door with a brass knocker, a bay window in the parlour, and water laid on to the kitchen sink. Plus the *éclat* of living in one of the villas.

Although the speculative builder had left the making of the back garden to his tenant, he had finished the small plot in front by laying a few feet of turf round a small centre flower bed. Ornate iron railings enclosed this small space and a red-and-blue-tiled path led up to the front door. Outside, at the edge of the sidewalk, young trees had been planted, of which some had already died and others were pining, but, lining the favourite and most built-up road, a sufficient number survived to give colour to its name of Chestnut Avenue.

In Laura's time, a few of the villas were occupied by ambitious Candleford Green families which had migrated; more had been taken by clerks and shopmen from Candleford town who fancied a country life or wished to reduce their rent. Six shillings a week for a five-roomed villa was certainly not excessive, but no doubt it repaid the builder-owner well enough for his outlay. Laura's uncle, who was also a builder in Candleford, declared that the villas were run up of old oddments of second-hand stuff, without proper foundations, and that the first high wind would blow half of them down; but his pessimism may have been due to professional rivalry, though, to do him justice, it must be said that he spoke the truth when he frowned and shook his head and declared: 'Never touch a cheap job. Not my line.'

Chestnut Avenue stood, apparently firmly, as long as Laura lived near and may quite probably be standing now, let at treble the rent to trebly paid wage-earners, with the chestnut trees fully grown and candled with blossoms and a wireless mast in every back garden. As they were built, almost before the paint was dry the villas were occupied and the new tenants tied back their lace curtains with blue or pink ribbon and painted on the gate the name of their choice: 'Chatsworth' or 'Naples' or 'Sunnyside' or 'Herne Bay'.

Laura, although conscious of disloyalty to 'the trade', personified for her by her father and uncle, still thought the Chestnut Avenue houses stylish. She had just enough taste, or sense of humour, to think some of the names chosen for them by the occupiers were unsuitable – 'Balmoral' was the latest addition – but she saw nothing amiss with the wide-ribbon pale blue or pink curtain ties, though she herself would have preferred green or yellow. Except for the ex-villagers whom she already knew, the villas were occupied by a class of people which was new to her, the lower fringe of the lower middle class, of which she was to see a great deal later.

Her first introduction to this, to her, new way of life she owed to a Mrs Green of 'The Shack', the wife of a clerk in the Candleford Post Office. She had come to know the husband in the way of business, he had introduced her to his wife, and an invitation to tea had followed.

217

The Greens' villa was only distinguishable from the others by its name and by the maidenhair fern which stood in place of the usual aspidistra on a little table exactly in the centre of the small space between the draped curtains at the parlour window. Mrs Green said aspidistras were common, and Laura soon discovered that she had a great dislike of common things and especially of common people. The people who lived next door, she told Laura, were 'awfully common'. The man was a jobbing gardener, 'a clodhopper' she called him, and his wife wore his cloth cap when she hung out her washing. They were toasting herrings, morning, noon, and night, and the smell was 'most offensive'. She thought the landlord ought to be more particular in choosing his tenants. Laura, who was used to the ways of those she called 'clodhoppers' and their wives, and herself enjoyed a good bloater toasted on the coals for supper, heard this with wonder. Of course men who worked on the land were common, there were so

many of them, but then there were a good many men in every other trade or calling, so why complain of the number? When it gradually dawned upon her that Mrs Green used the word 'common' in a social sense, she was rather afraid that she would be thought common, too; but she need not have feared, for that lady did not think of her at all, excepting as the possessor of eyes and ears.

Mrs Green was a small, fair woman, still under thirty, who would have been pretty had not her face habitually worn a worried expression which sharpened her features and was already destroying her bloom. Her refinement, or perhaps her means, did not run to visits to a dentist and, to hide decaying teeth, she cultivated a thin, close-lipped little smile. But her hair was still very pretty and beautifully cared for, and she had pretty hands which she rubbed with cold cream after washing the tea things.

Her husband was also small and fair, but his manners were more simple and his expression was opener and franker than that of his wife. When he laughed he laughed loudly, and then his wife would look at him reproachfully and say in a pained voice, '*Al*bert' He had not had the same training in the art of keeping up appearances as his wife, for while she, as she said, had come down in the world, having been born into what she vaguely termed 'a refined family', he had begun to earn his living as a telegraph messenger and worked his way up to his present position, which, though still modest, was in those days something of an achievement. Left to himself, he would have been a pleasant, homely kind of fellow who would have enjoyed working in his garden and afterwards sitting down in his shirtsleeves to a bloater or tinned salmon for tea. But he had married a genteel wife and she had educated him as far as possible up to her own standard.

They were both touchingly proud of their home, and Laura on her first visit had to be shown every nook and corner of it, including the inside of the cupboards. It was furnished in accord with its architectural style. The parlour, which they called the 'drawing-room', had a complete suite of furniture upholstered in green tapestry, and there was a green carpet, but not quite the right shade of green, on the floor. Photographs in ornate frames stood on little tables and a set of framed pictures on the walls illustrated the courtship of an insipid looking couple – 'Lovers' Meeting', 'The Letter', 'Lovers' Quarrel', and 'Wedded'. There was not a book or a flower in the room and not so much as a cushion awry to show that it was lived in. As a matter of fact, it was not. It was more a museum or a temple or a furniture showroom than a living-room. They sat in state in the bay window on Sunday evenings and watched their neighbours pass by, but took their meals and spent the rest of their time in the kitchen, which was a much pleasanter room. . . .

Everything was beautifully kept, furniture and floors were highly polished, windows gleamed, curtains and counterpanes were immaculate, and the little kitchen at the back of the house was a model of neatness. Laura found out afterwards that Mrs Green worked herself nearly to death. With only one child and a house only a little larger than theirs, she worked twice the number of hours and spent ten times the energy of the cottage women. They, standing at their doors with their arms folded, enjoying a gossip with a neighbour, would often complain that a woman's work was never done; but the Mrs Greens were working away while they gossiped and, afterwards, when they were indoors having 'a set down with a cup o' tay', the Mrs Greens, wearing gloves, were polishing the silver. For, of course, forks and spoons and any other metal objects possessed by a Green housewife were known collectively as 'the silver', even if there was not one single hallmark to be seen upon any of them. . . .

Her acquaintance with the Greens brought Laura for the first time in contact with the kind of people among whom much of her life was to be spent. It was a class newly emerging in this country, on the borderline between the working and middle classes. Its main type had many good points. Those belonging to it were industrious, frugal and home-loving. Their houses were well kept, their incomes well managed, and their ambitions on their children's behalf knew no bounds. No sacrifice on the part of the parents was too great if, by it, they could give a better start in life than their own to their offspring. The average number of children in a family was two, but there were many only children and nearly as many childless homes; a family of three was unusual.

The men's suits were kept well brushed, sponged and pressed by their wives, and the women had the knack of dressing well on little. Many of them were able to make, alter, and bring up to date their own clothes. They were good cooks and managers; their homes, though often tasteless, were substantially furnished and beautifully kept; and, although when alone they might take their meals in the kitchen, they had elaborate afternoon teacloths and fashionable knick-knacks for the table for festive occasions.

Those were the lines along which they were developing. Spiritually, they had lost ground, rather than gained it. Their working-class forefathers had had religious or political ideals; their talk had not lost the raciness of the soil and was seasoned with native wit which, if sometimes crude, was authentic. Few of this section of their sons and daughters were churchgoers, or gave much thought to religious matters. When the subject of religion was mentioned, they professed to subscribe to its dogmas and to be

shocked at the questioning of the most outworn of these; but, in reality, their creed was that of keeping up appearances. The reading they did was mass reading. Before they would open a book, they had to be told it was one that everybody was reading. The works of Marie Corelli and Nat Gould were immensely popular with them. They had not sufficient sense of humour to originate it, but borrowed it from music-hall turns and comic papers, and the voice in which such gems were repeated was flat and toneless compared to the old country speech.

But those who had left village life and all it stood for behind them were few compared to the number of those who stayed at home and waited for change to come to them. Change came slowly, if surely, and right into the early years of this century many of the old village ways of living remained and those who cherished the old customs were much as country people had been for generations. A little better educated, a little more democratic, a little more prosperous than their parents had been, but still the same unpretentious, warm-hearted people, with just enough malice to give point to their wit and a growing sense of injustice

which was making them begin to inquire when their turn would come to enjoy a fair share of the fruits of the earth they tilled.

They, too, or, rather, their children and grandchildren, were to come in time to the parting of the ways when the choice would have to be made between either merging themselves in the mass standardization of a new civilization or adapting the best of the new to their own needs while still retaining those qualities and customs which have given country life its distinctive character. That choice may not even now have been determined.

But only a few of the wisest foresaw that the need for such a choice would arise when, for Laura, what appeared to be an opportunity offered and, driven on by well-meant advice from without and from within by the restless longing of youth to see and experience the whole of life, she disappeared from the country scene. To return often, but never as herself part of it, for she could only be that in her native county, where she had sprung from the soil.

On the last morning of her postwoman's round, when she came to the path between trees where she had seen the birds' footprints on the snow, she turned and looked back upon the familiar landmarks. It was a morning of ground mist, yellow sunshine, and high rifts of blue, white-cloud-dappled sky. The leaves were still thick on the trees, but dew-spangled gossamer threads hung on the bushes and the shrill little cries of unrest of the swallows skimming the green open spaces of the park told of autumn and change.

There was the stable tower with its clock-face and, near it, though unseen, was the courtyard where she had been annoyed – foolishly annoyed, she thought now – by the horseplay of the footmen. The chief offenders had gone long before and with those who had taken their places she knew quite well how to deal, even if they had been offensive, which they were not, for she was nearly three years older. There, where the path wound past the two copses, she had met Philip White – he, too, had left the estate – and away to the left were the meadows where the cows had obstructed her path. Farther on, quite out of sight, was the Post Office where, doubtless, Miss Lane was at that moment dispensing stamps with the air of a high priestess, still a little offended by what she considered Laura's desertion, but not too much so to have promised her as a parting gift one of her own watches and chains. And around the Post Office and green was the village where she had had good times and times not so good and had come to know every one of its inhabitants and to count most of them as her friends.

Nearer at hand were the trees and bushes and wild-flower patches beside the path she had trodden daily. The pond where the yellow brandyball waterlilies grew, the little birch thicket where the long-tailed tits had congregated, the boathouse where she had sheltered from the thunderstorm and seen the rain plash like leaden bullets into the leaden water, and the hillock beyond from which she had seen the perfect rainbow. She was never to see any of these again, but she was to carry a mental picture of them, to be recalled at will, through the changing scenes of a lifetime.

As she went on her way, gossamer threads, spun from bush to bush, barricaded her pathway, and as she broke through one after another of these fairy barricades she thought, 'They're trying to bind and keep me.' But the threads which were to bind her to her native county were more enduring than gossamer. They were spun of love and kinship and cherished memories.

A note about the text: *Lark Rise to Candleford* comprises three books published separately between 1939 and 1943. In abridging the text for this one-volume edition it has been possible to avoid a number of overlaps and repetitions which were necessary in the three separate books, and to omit some descriptive passages designed to set the scene for new readers of the second and third volumes. But to contain the book within its present compass other deletions were necessary.

It is in *Lark Rise*, her first volume, that Flora Thompson paints the most vivid portrait of the old countryside, and the way of life which was already disappearing as she herself grew up. These chapters have been abridged much less than the second two volumes, in which Laura ventures into the grown-up, and to us more familiar, world of Candleford.

All omissions in the text have been indicated by the insertion of three full points.

Illustration sources and acknowledgements: Abbreviations: BAL Bridgeman Art Library; CW Christopher Wood Gallery, London; ETA ET Archive; FAPL Fine Art Picture Library; FAS Fine Art Society, London; HCL Hereford City Library; HPL BBC Hulton Picture Library; MERL Museum of English Rural Life, Reading; OCL Oxford Central Library; OCM Oxfordshire County Museums Service; SB Sotheby's Belgravia; V&A Victoria and Albert Museum, London; WAG Wolverhampton Art Gallery.

Page 3 Sir George Clausen, 'Building the Rick' (Birmingham Museum & Art Gallery); 9 Helen Allingham, 'Redlynch' (CW); 10 Noke, Oxon (OCM); 12 Child with sheep (MERL); 13 Clausen, 'The Allotment Garden' (FAS); 16 Allingham, 'Washing Day' (FAPL); 19 Leazing (MERL); 20 C.E. Wilson, 'A Saucer of Milk' (FAPL); 21 Grundy's English Views, Marbles (HPL); 23 Allingham, 'Gathering Firewood' (FAPL); 29 Children (HPL); 30 Allingham 'Watching a Kitten' (FAPL); 31 On a stile (Mansell Collection); 35 Clausen, 'The Mowers' (BAL/Usher Gallery, Lincoln); 36 Man with sickle (MERL/HCL); 38 A.A. Glendening, 'Harvesting' (FAPL); 41 Ploughing (MERL/Ransome Collection); 43 Clausen, 'December' (BAL/private collection); 44 Threshing (MERL); 45 Harvesting near Henley (OCL); 47 Allingham, 'Tired Out' (ETA); 48 Farrier (MERL); 50 G.V. Cole, 'Harvest Time' (BAL/City of Bristol Museum and Art Gallery); 52 A close game (HPL); 56 Old Dorchester lady (OCL); 58 Berkshire shepherd (OCL); 59 Claude Strachan, 'Feeding the Doves' (CW); 61 Tradesman delivering goods (MERL); 62 Myles Birket Foster, 'The Lacemaker' (FAPL); 64 Benny Knight at Will Hall Farm (MERL/Hampshire County Museums Service); 67 Wilson, 'Beehives' (CW); 71 Allingham, 'Old Cottage at Witley' (SB); 72 Cowman (MERL); 73 Carting faggots (MERL); 75 Clausen, 'The Girl at the Gate' (Tate Gallery); 78 Thomas Tyndale, 'A West Sussex Cottage' (CW); 81 Skep (MERL/HCL); 83 Birket Foster, 'A Quiet Afternoon' (FAPL); 91 Clausen, 'In the Orchard' (BAL/Salford Art Gallery); 92 May garlands at Iffley (OCL); 93 School group at Combe, Oxon (OCM); 94 Allingham, 'Bluebells' (FAPL); 98 Children of Garsington, Oxon (OCL); 99 E.M. Waite, 'Beechwoods in May' (FAPL); 102 Allingham, 'The Cuckoo' (ETA/V&A); 104 Scythe-sharpening at Wilcroft (MERL/HCL); 106 George Shalders, 'Shepherd and Sheep' (CW); 108 Children of Garsington (OCL); 111 B. Edward Warren, 'Solitude' (FAPL); 115 Wilson, 'Between School Hours' (FAPL); 116 Blacksmiths (OCL); 117 Horse-drawn reaper (OCL); 119 Clausen, 'Bird Scaring' (BAL/Harris Museum, Preston); 123 T.F. Marshall, 'May Day Garlands' (CW); 127 Glendening, 'Cornfield in Kent' (FAPL); 130 J.T. Linnell, 'The Sheepfold – Morning in Autumn' (BAL/WAG); 132 Pillars of the church (OCL); 133 And so to church (HPL); 135 Clausen, 'The Gleaners Returning' (Tate Gallery); 139 Clausen 'October Morning' (BAL/private collection); 140 Haymaking at Hethe, Oxon (OCM); 141 Haymaking at Garsington (OCL); 146 Feeding the pig (MERL); 147 Allingham, 'Cottage at Chiddingfold' (ETA/V&A); 148 Grundy, Domestic servants (HPL); 149 Grundy, Making butter (HPL); 150 Frank Bramley, 'At the End of the Day' (FAPL); 157 Allingham, 'Cottage' (CW); 158 Charlbury (OCL); 160 A.C. Cooke, 'Domestic Lesson' (BAL); 163 H.H. La Thangue, 'Cutting Bracken' (FAPL); 164 Standlake village band (OCL); 169 Wilson, 'Outside a Cottage' (FAPL); 174 The forge at Fringford (OCL); 175 La Thangue, 'Leaving Home' (FAS/FORBES Magazine Collection, New York); 180 J.H. Hooper, 'A Hillside Cornfield' (FAPL); 183 Glendening, 'The Cabbage Patch' (FAPL); 186 Shelsbury road, Charlbury (OCL); 187 The green, Standlake (OCL); 189 Lilian Stannard, 'Old Thatched Summerhouse' (BAL/CW); 193 F.D. Hardy, 'Posting a Letter' (BAL/CW); 195 Charlbury street scene (OCL); 197 Allingham, 'Primrose Copse' (CW); 198 Farmyard near Wincanton (MERL/Professor John Read Collection); 200 Allingham, 'A Kentish Cottage' (SB); 202 Bicester meet (HPL); 203 Anon, 'Haymaking' (FAPL); 207 Allingham, 'A Berkshire Cottage' (FAPL); 211 Elizabeth Stanhope Forbes, 'The Edge of the Woods' (BAL/WAG); 212 Grundy, Gamekeeper (HPL); 213 Geese (HPL); 217 Allingham, 'Cottage near Wells' (FAPL); 218 The pump (OCL); 220 Grundy, Blacksmith's forge (HPL); 221 Thomas Mackay, 'Riverside Scene' (CW). Grateful acknowledgement is also made: to Tony Evans for photographing the front cover label; to the Trustees of the Estate of Sir George Clausen; to Lilian Freeman, Jessie Parkes and Molly Wood for the supply of pressed flowers; and to Malcolm Graham, Christine Bloxham, Dr Sadie Ward, Peyton Skipwith, Christopher Wood, Harriet Bridgeman and Trevor Peacock for their assistance in various ways with picture research. The woodcuts illustrating chapter headings are by Thomas Bewick.